DITED AND W

RUDYARD KIPLING

Modern Critical Views

These and other titles in preparation

Modern Critical Views

RUDYARD KIPLING

Edited and with an introduction by

Harold Bloom
Sterling Professor of the Humanities
Yale University

CHELSEA HOUSE PUBLISHERS ◇ 1987
New York ◇ New Haven ◇ Philadelphia

© 1987 by Chelsea House Publishers, a division
of Chelsea House Educational Communications, Inc.,
   95 Madison Avenue, New York, NY 10016
   345 Whitney Avenue, New Haven, CT 06511
   5014 West Chester Pike, Edgemont, PA 19028

Introduction © 1987 by Harold Bloom

Printed and bound in the United States of America

∞ The paper used in this publication meets the minimum
requirements of the American National Standard for
Permanence of Paper for Printed Library Materials,
Z39.48-1984.

Library of Congress Cataloging-in-Publication Data
Rudyard Kipling.
      (Modern critical views)
      Bibliography: p.
      Includes index.
      Contents: On preparing to read Kipling / Randall
Jarrell—Kim and the stories / Angus Wilson—The
pleasures of Kim / Irving Howe—[etc.]
   1. Kipling, Rudyard, 1865–1932—Criticism and
interpretation.   I. Bloom, Harold.   II. Title.
III. Series.
PR4857.R77   1987   828'.809   86-21578
ISBN 0-87754-646-0 (alk. paper)

Contents

Editor's Note

This book brings together a representative selection of the best criticism available upon the writings of Rudyard Kipling. The essays are reprinted here in the chronological order of their original publication. I am grateful to Peter Childers for his skill and devotion in helping me edit this volume.

My introduction first suggests that Kipling, despite appearances, had a profound affinity to the aesthetic vision and solipsistic nihilism of Walter Pater, and then traces both these qualities and their antitheses in *Kim*, Kipling's strongest single work. The chronological sequence of criticism begins with Randall Jarrell's overview of Kipling's achievement as a story writer, which is followed here by two loving appreciations of *Kim*, by the British novelist Angus Wilson and by Irving Howe. Donald Davie, poet and critic, reconsiders Kipling's imperialism as a mode of puritanism, while Zohreh T. Sullivan subtly unveils the sexual anxieties and divided loyalties that help to constitute the literary aspects of that imperialism.

In what seems to me a breakthrough into a new mode of Kipling criticism, David Bromwich brings together two of the best stories, "Wireless" and "Dayspring Mishandled," with the best poems and *Kim* so as to illuminate the daemonic basis of Kipling's art. Elliot L. Gilbert relates the death of Kipling's son in World War I to the poet-novelist's later art and life, both of which invest deeply in a certain metaphoric silence. In this book's final essay, Robert L. Caserio reads *The Light That Failed* as Kipling's deliberate poetics of failure, and speculates in regard to Kipling's influence upon Conrad. Caserio, like Bromwich and Gilbert, teaches us that there is still a largely unknown and profound writer to be uncovered in Kipling.

Introduction

I

Twenty years after writing his essay of 1943 on Kipling (reprinted in *The Liberal Imagination*, 1951), Lionel Trilling remarked that if he could write the critique again, he would do it "less censoriously and with more affectionate admiration." Trilling, always the representative critic of his era, reflected a movement in the evaluation of Kipling that still continues in 1987. I suspect that this movement will coexist with its dialectical countermovement, of recoil against Kipling, as long as our literary tradition lasts. Kipling is an authentically *popular* writer, in every sense of the word. Stories like "The Man Who Would Be King"; children's tales from *The Jungle Books* and the *Just So Stories*; the novel *Kim*, which is clearly Kipling's masterwork; certain late stories and dozens of ballads—these survive both as high literature and as perpetual entertainment. It is as though Kipling had set out to refute the Sublime function of literature, which is to make us forsake easier pleasures for more difficult pleasures.

In his speech on "Literature," given in 1906, Kipling sketched a dark tale of the storyteller's destiny:

> There is an ancient legend which tells us that when a man first achieved a most notable deed he wished to explain to his Tribe what he had done. As soon as he began to speak, however, he was smitten with dumbness, he lacked words, and sat down. Then there arose—according to the story—a masterless man, one who had taken no part in the action of his fellow, who had no special virtues, but who was afflicted—that is the phrase—with the magic of the necessary word. He saw; he told; he described the merits of the notable deed in such a fashion, we are assured, that the words "became alive and walked up and down in the hearts of all his hearers." Thereupon, the Tribe seeing that the

1

words were certainly alive, and fearing lest the man with the words would hand down untrue tales about them to their children, took and killed him. But, later, they saw that the magic was in the words, not in the man.

Seven years later, in the ghastly Primal History Scene of *Totem and Taboo*'s fourth chapter, Freud depicted a curiously parallel scene, where a violent primal father is murdered and devoured by his sons, who thus bring to an end the patriarchal horde. Kipling's Primal Storytelling Scene features "a masterless man" whose only virtue is "the necessary word." But he too is slain by the Tribe or primal horde, lest he transmit fictions about the Tribe to its children. Only later, in Freud, do the sons of the primal father experience remorse, and so "the dead father became stronger than the living one had been." Only later, in Kipling, does the Tribe see "that the magic was in the words, not in the man."

Freud's true subject, in his Primal History Scene, was the transference, the carrying-over from earlier to later attachments of an over-determined affect. The true subject of Kipling's Primal Storytelling Scene is not so much the Tale of the Tribe, or the magic that was in the words, but the storyteller's freedom, the masterless man's vocation that no longer leads to death, but that can lead to a death-in-life. What Kipling denies is his great fear, which is that the magic indeed is just as much in the masterless man as it is in the words.

Kipling, with his burly imperialism and his indulgences in anti-intellectualism, would seem at first out of place in the company of Walter Pater, Oscar Wilde, and William Butler Yeats. Nevertheless, Kipling writes in the rhetorical stance of an aesthete, and is very much a Paterian in the metaphysical sense. The "Conclusion" to Pater's *Renaissance* is precisely the credo of Kipling's protagonists:

> Not to discriminate every moment some passionate attitude in those about us, and in the brilliancy of their gifts some tragic dividing of forces on their ways, is, on this short day of frost and sun, to sleep before evening. With this sense of the splendour of our experience and of its awful brevity, gathering all we are into one desperate effort to see and touch, we shall hardly have time to make theories about the things we see and touch. What we have to do is to be for ever curiously testing new opinions and courting new impressions.

Frank Kermode observed that Kipling was a writer "who steadfastly preferred action and machinery to the prevalent Art for Art's Sake," but that is to misread weakly what Pater meant by ending the "Conclusion" to *The Renaissance* with what soon became a notorious formula:

> We have an interval, and then our place knows us no more. Some spend this interval in listlessness, some in high passions, the wisest, at least among "the children of this world," in art and song. For our one chance lies in expanding that interval, in getting as many pulsations as possible into the given time. Great passions may give us this quickened sense of life, ecstasy and sorrow of love, the various forms of enthusiastic activity, disinterested or otherwise, which come naturally to many of us. Only be sure it is passion—that it does yield you this fruit of a quickened, multiplied consciousness. Of this wisdom, the poetic passion, the desire of beauty, the love of art for art's sake, has most; for art comes to you professing frankly to give nothing but the highest quality to your moments as they pass, and simply for those moments' sake.

Like Pater, like Nietzsche, Kipling sensed that we possess and cherish fictions because the reductive truth would destroy us. "The love of art for art's sake" simply means that we choose to believe in a fiction, while knowing that it is not true, to adopt Wallace Stevens's version of the Paterian credo. And fiction, according to Kipling, was written by daemonic forces within us, by "some tragic dividing of forces on their ways." Those forces are no more meaningful than the tales and ballads they produce. What Kipling shares finally with Pater is a deep conviction that we are caught always in a vortex of sensations, a solipsistic concourse of impressions piling upon one another, with great vividness but little consequence.

II

Kipling's authentic precursor and literary hero was Mark Twain, whose *Huckleberry Finn* and *Tom Sawyer* are reflected inescapably in *Kim*, certainly Kipling's finest achievement. "An Interview with Mark Twain" records Kipling's vision of the two hours of genial audience granted him, starting with Twain's:

> "Well, you think you owe me something, and you've come to tell me so. That's what I call squaring a debt handsomely."

Kim, permanent work as it is, does not square the debt, partly because Kim is, as David Bromwich notes, both Huck Finn and Tom Sawyer, which is to confuse essentially opposed personalities. Since *Kim* is founded upon *Huckleberry Finn*, and not on *Don Quixote*, the mixing of Huck and Tom in Kim's nature brings about a softening of focus that malforms the novel. We cannot find Sancho Panza in Kim, though there is a touch of the Don, as well as of Nigger Jim, in the lama. Insofar as he is free but lonely, Kim is Huck; insofar as he serves the worldly powers, he is Tom. It is striking that in his "Interview with Mark Twain," Kipling expresses interest only in Tom Sawyer, asking Twain "whether we were ever going to hear of Tom Sawyer as a man." I suspect that some anxiety of influence was involved, since *Kim* is the son of the *Adventures of Huckleberry Finn* and not of the lesser novel.

Kim is one of the great instances in the language of a popular adventure story that is also exalted literature. *Huckleberry Finn* is too astonishing a book, too nearly the epic of the American consciousness, together with *Leaves of Grass* and *Moby-Dick*, to be regarded as what it only pretends to be: a good yarn. *Kim* stations itself partly in that mode which ranges from Rider Haggard, at its nadir, to Robert Louis Stevenson, at its zenith: the boy's romance crossing over into the ancient form of romance proper.

There are many splendors in *Kim*, but the greatest is surely the relation between Kim and his master, the lovable, half-mad Tibetan lama, who proves to be Kim's true father, and to whom Kim becomes the best of sons. It is a triumph of the exact representation of profound human affection, rather than a sentimentality of any kind, that can move us to tears as the book ends:

> "Hear me! I bring news! The Search is finished. Comes now the Reward: . . . Thus. When we were among the Hills, I lived on thy strength till the young branch bowed and nigh broke. When we came out of the Hills, I was troubled for thee and for other matters which I held in my heart. The boat of my soul lacked direction; I could not see into the Cause of Things. So I gave thee over to the virtuous woman altogether. I took no food. I drank no water. Still I saw not the Way. They pressed food upon me and cried at my shut door. So I removed myself to a hollow under a tree. I took no food. I took no water. I sat in meditation two days and two nights, abstracting my mind; inbreathing and outbreathing in the required manner. . . . Upon the second night—so great was my reward—the wise Soul loosed itself from the silly Body and went free. This I have never before attained, though I have stood on the threshold of it. Consider, for it is a marvel!"

"A marvel indeed. Two days and two nights without food! Where was the Sahiba?" said Kim under his breath.

"Yea, my Soul went free, and, wheeling like an eagle, saw indeed that there was no Teshoo Lama nor any other soul. As a drop draws to water, so my soul drew near to the Great Soul which is beyond all things. At that point, exalted in contemplation, I saw all Hind, from Ceylon in the sea to the Hills, and my own Painted Rocks at Such-zen; I saw every camp and village, to the least, where we have ever rested. I saw them at one time and in one place; for they were within the Soul. By this I knew the Soul had passed beyond the illusion of Time and Space and of Things. By this I knew that I was free. I saw thee lying in thy cot, and I saw thee falling down hill under the idolater—at one time, in one place, in my Soul, which, as I say, had touched the Great Soul. Also I saw the stupid body of Teshoo Lama lying down, and the *hakim* from Dacca kneeled beside, shouting in its ear. Then my Soul was all alone, and I saw nothing, for I was all things, having reached the Great Soul. And I meditated a thousand years, passionless, well aware of the Causes of all Things. Then a voice cried: 'What shall come to the boy if thou art dead?' and I was shaken back and forth in myself with pity for thee; and I said: 'I will return to my *chela*, lest he miss the Way.' Upon this my Soul, which is the soul of Teshoo Lama, withdrew itself from the Great Soul with strivings and yearnings and retchings and agonies not to be told. As the egg from the fish, as the fish from the water, as the water from the cloud, as the cloud from the thick air, so put forth, so leaped out, so drew away, so fumed up the soul of Teshoo Lama from the Great Soul. Then a voice cried: 'The River! Take heed to the River!' and I looked down upon all the world, which was as I had seen it before—one in time, one in place—and I saw plainly the River of the Arrow at my feet. At that hour my Soul was hampered by some evil or other whereof I was not wholly cleansed, and it lay upon my arms and coiled round my waist; but I put it aside, and I cast forth as an eagle in my flight for the very place of the River. I pushed aside world upon world for thy sake. I saw the River below me—the River of the Arrow—and, descending, the waters of it closed over me; and behold I was again in the body of Teshoo Lama, but free from sin, and the *hakim* from Dacca bore up my head in the waters of the River. It is here! It is behind the mango-tope here—even here!"

"Allah Kerim! Oh, well that the Babu was by! Wast thou very
wet?"

"Why should I regard? I remember the *hakim* was concerned
for the body of Teshoo Lama. He haled it out of the holy water
in his hands, and there came afterwards thy horse-seller from the
North with a cot and men, and they put the body on the cot and
bore it up to the Sahiba's house."

"What said the Sahiba?"

"I was meditating in that body, and did not hear. So thus the
Search is ended. For the merit that I have acquired, the River of
the Arrow is here. It broke forth at our feet, as I have said. I
have found it. Son of my Soul, I have wrenched my Soul back
from the Threshold of Freedom to free thee from all sin—as I
am free, and sinless. Just is the Wheel! Certain is our deliverance.
Come!"

He crossed his hands on his lap and smiled, as a man may who
has won Salvation for himself and his beloved.

This long passage builds, through radiant apprehensions, to an extraordinarily controlled and calm epiphany of parental love. The vision of the
lama, though it presents itself as the wise soul's freedom from the silly body,
is clearly not dualistic, but is caused by the lama's honest declaration: "I
was troubled for thee." Caught up in the freedom from illusion, and free
therefore supposedly of any concern for other souls, since, like one's own,
they are not, the lama is close to the final freedom: "for I was all things."
The voice that cries him back to life is the voice of his fatherly love for Kim,
and the reward for his return to existence, negating mystical transport, is
his true vision of the River, goal of his quest. It breaks forth at his feet, and
is better than freedom, because it is not merely solitary, but is Salvation for
his beloved adopted son, as well as for himself.

Certainly this is Kipling's most humane and hopeful moment, normative
and positive. *Kim* is, like its more masterly precursor work, *Huckleberry Finn*,
a book that returns us to the central values, avoiding those shadows of the
abyss that hover uneasily elsewhere in Kipling. Yet even here the darker
and truer Kipling lingers, in the sudden vision of nothingness that Kim
experiences, only a few pages before his final reunion with the lama:

At first his legs bent like bad pipe-stems, and the flood and rush
of the sunlit air dazzled him. He squatted by the white wall, the
mind rummaging among the incidents of the long *dooli* journey,
the lama's weaknesses, and, now that the stimulus of talk was

removed, his own self-pity, of which, like the sick, he had great store. The unnerved brain edged away from all the outside, as a raw horse, once rowelled, sidles from the spur. It was enough, amply enough, that the spoil of the *kilta* was away—off his hands—out of his possession. He tried to think of the lama,—to wonder why he had tumbled into a brook,—but the bigness of the world, seen between the forecourt gates, swept linked thought aside. Then he looked upon the trees and the broad fields, with the thatched huts hidden among crops—looked with strange eyes unable to take up the size and proportion and use of things— stared for a still half-hour. All that while he felt, though he could not put it into words, that his soul was out of gear with its surroundings—a cog-wheel unconnected with any machinery, just like the idle cog-wheel of a cheap Beheea sugar-crusher laid by in a corner. The breezes fanned over him, the parrots shrieked at him, the noises of the populated house behind—squabbles, orders, and reproofs—hit on dead ears.

"I am Kim. I am Kim. And what is Kim?" His soul repeated it again and again.

Despite the Indian imagery and the characteristic obsession of Kipling with machinery, the mark of Walter Pater's aesthetic impressionism, with its sensations beckoning us to the abyss, is clearly set upon this passage. Identity flees with the flux of impressions, and the dazzlement of "the flood and rush of the sunlit air" returns us to the cosmos of the "Conclusion" to *The Renaissance*. Kipling's art, in *Kim*, is after all art for art's sake, in the dark predicate that there is nothing else. The extravagant fiction of the great love between an Irish boy gone native in India, half a Huck Finn enthralled with freedom and half a Tom Sawyer playing games with authority, and a quixotic, aged Tibetan lama is Kipling's finest invention, and moves us endlessly. But how extravagant a fiction it is, and had to be! Kipling refused to profess the faith of those who live and die for and by art, yet in the end he had no other faith.

RANDALL JARRELL

On Preparing to Read Kipling

Mark Twain said that it isn't what they don't know that hurts people, it's what they do know that isn't so. This is true of Kipling. If people don't know about Kipling they can read Kipling, and then they'll know about Kipling: it's ideal. But most people already do know about Kipling—not very much, but too much: they know what isn't so, or what might just as well not be so, it matters so little. They know that, just as Calvin Coolidge's preacher was against sin and the Snake was for it, Kipling was for imperialism; he talked about the white man's burden; he was a crude popular—immensely popular—writer who got popular by writing "If," and "On the Road to Mandalay," and *The Jungle Book*, and stories about India like Somerset Maugham, and children's stories; he wrote "East is East and West is West and never the twain shall meet"; he wrote, "The female of the species is more deadly than the male"—or was that Pope? *Somebody* wrote it. In short: Kipling was someone people used to think was wonderful, but we know better than that now.

People certainly didn't know better than that then. "Dear Harry," William James begins. (It is hard to remember, hard to believe, that anyone ever called Henry James *Harry*, but if it had to be done, William James was the right man to do it.) "Last Sunday I dined with Howells at the Childs', and was delighted to hear him say that you were both a friend and an admirer of Rudyard Kipling. I am ashamed to say that I have been ashamed to write of that infant phenomenon, not knowing, with your exquisitely refined taste,

From *Kipling, Auden & Co.: Essays and Reviews, 1935–1964*. © 1961 by Mrs. Randall Jarrell. Farrar, Straus & Giroux, 1961.

how you might be affected by him and fearing to *jar*. [It is wonderful *to have the engineer / Hoist with his own petard*.] The more rejoiced am I at this, but why didn't you say so ere now? He's more of a Shakespeare than anyone yet in this generation of ours, as it strikes me. And seeing the new effects he lately brings in in *The Light That Failed*, and that Simla Ball story with Mrs. Hauksbee in the *Illustrated London News*, makes one sure now that he is only at the beginning of a rapidly enlarging career, with indefinite growth before him. Much of his present coarseness and jerkiness is youth only, divine youth. But *what* a youth! Distinctly the biggest literary phenomenon of our time. He has such human entrails, and he takes less time to get under the heartstrings of his personages than anyone I know. On the whole, bless him.

"All intellectual work is the same,—the artist feeds the public on his own bleeding insides. Kant's *Kritik* is just like a Strauss waltz, and I felt the other day, finishing *The Light That Failed*, and an ethical address to be given at Yale College simultaneously, that there was no *essential* difference between Rudyard Kipling and myself as far as that sacrificial element goes."

It surprises us to have James take Kipling so seriously, without reservations, with Shakespeare—to treat him as if he were Kant's *Kritik* and not a Strauss waltz. (Even Henry James, who could refer to "the good little Thomas Hardy"—who was capable of applying to the Trinity itself the adjective *poor*—somehow felt that he needed for Kipling that coarse word *genius*, and called him, at worst, "the great little Kipling.") Similarly, when Goethe and Matthew Arnold write about Byron, we are surprised to see them bringing in Shakespeare—are surprised to see how unquestioningly, with what serious respect, they speak of Byron, as if he were an ocean or a new ice age: "our soul," wrote Arnold, "had *felt* him like the thunder's roll." It is as though mere common sense, common humanity, required this of them: the existence of a world figure like Byron demands (as the existence of a good or great writer does not) that any inhabitant of the world treat him somehow as the world treats him. Goethe knew that Byron "is a child when he reflects," but this did not prevent him from treating Byron exactly as he treated that other world figure Napoleon.

An intelligent man said that the world felt Napoleon as a weight, and that when he died it would give a great *oof* of relief. This is just as true of Byron, or of such Byrons of their days as Kipling and Hemingway: after a generation or two the world is tired of being their pedestal, shakes them off with an *oof*, and then—hoisting onto its back a new world figure—feels the penetrating satisfaction of having made a mistake all its own. Then for a generation or two the Byron lies in the dust where we left him: if the old world did him more than justice, a new one does him less. "If he was so good as all that, why isn't he still famous?" the new world asks—if it asks anything. And then when another generation or two are done, we decide that he wasn't altogether a mistake people made in those days, but a real writer after all—that if we like *Childe Harold* a good deal less than anyone thought of liking it then, we like *Don Juan* a good deal more. Byron *was* a writer, people just didn't realize the sort of writer he was. We can feel impatient with Byron's world for liking him for the wrong reasons, and with the succeeding world for disliking him for the wrong reasons, and we are glad that our world, the real world, has at last settled Byron's account.

Kipling's account is still unsettled. Underneath, we still hold it against him that the world quoted him in its sleep, put him in its headlines when he was ill, acted as if he were God; we are glad that we have Hemingway instead, to put in *our* headlines when his plane crashes. Kipling is in the dust, and the dust seems to us a very good place for him. But in twenty or thirty years, when Hemingway is there instead, and we have a new Byron-Kipling-Hemingway to put in our news programs when his rocket crashes, our resistance to Hemingway will have taken the place of our resistance to Kipling, and we shall find ourselves willing to entertain the possibility that Kipling *was* a writer after all—people just didn't realize the sort of writer he was.

There is a way of traveling into this future—of realizing, now, the sort of writer Kipling was—that is unusually simple, but that people are unusually unwilling to take. The way is: to read Kipling as if one were not prepared to read Kipling; as if one didn't already know about Kipling—had never been told how readers do feel about Kipling, should feel about Kipling; as if one were setting out, naked, to see something that is there naked. I don't entirely blame the reader if he answers: "Thanks very much; if it's just the same to you, I'll keep my clothes on." It's only human of him—man is the animal that wears clothes. Yet aren't works of art in some sense a way of doing without clothes, a means by which reader, writer, and subject are able for once to accept their own nakedness? the nakedness not merely of the "naked truth," but also of the naked wishes that come before and after that truth? To read Kipling, for once, not as the crudely effective, popular writer we know him to be, but as, perhaps, the something else that even crudely effective, popular writers can become, would be to exhibit a magnanimity that might do justice both to Kipling's potentialities and to our own. Kipling did have, at first, the "coarseness and jerkiness" and mannered vanity of youth, human youth; Kipling did begin as a reporter, did print in newspapers the *Plain Tales from the Hills* which ordinary readers—and, unfortunately, most extraordinary ones—do think typical of his work; but then for half a century he kept writing. Chekhov began by writing jokes for magazines, skits for vaudeville; Shakespeare began by writing *Titus Andronicus* and *The Two Gentlemen of Verona*, some of the crudest plays any crudely effective, popular writer has ever turned out. Kipling is neither a Chekhov nor a Shakespeare, but he is far closer to both than to the clothing-store-dummy-with-the-solar-topee we have agreed to call Kipling. Kipling, like it or not, admit it or not, was a great genius; and a great neurotic; and a great professional, one of the most skillful writers who have ever existed—one of the writers who have used English best, one of the writers who most often have made other writers exclaim, in the queer tone they use for the exclamation: "Well, I've got to admit it really is *written*." When he died and was buried in that foreign land England, that only the Anglo-Indians know, I wish that they had put above his grave, there in *their* Westminster Abbey: "It really was *written*."

Mies Van Der Rohe said, very beautifully: "I don't want to be interesting, I want to be good." Kipling, a great realist but a greater inventor, could have said that he didn't want to be realistic, he wanted to get it right: that he wanted it not the way it did or—statistics show—does happen, but the way it really would happen. You often feel about something in Shakespeare or Dostoevsky that nobody ever said such a thing, but it's just the sort of thing people would say if they could—is more real, in some sense, than what people do say. If you have given your imagination free rein, let things go as far as they want to go, the world they made for themselves while you watched can have, for you and later watchers, a spontaneous finality. Some of Kipling has this spontaneous finality; and because he has written so many different kinds of stories—no writer of fiction of comparable genius has depended so much, for so long, on short stories alone—you end dazzled by his variety of realization: so many plants, and so many of them dewy!

If I had to pick one writer to invent a conversation between an animal, a god, and a machine, it would be Kipling. To discover what, if they ever said, the dumb would say—this takes real imagination; and this imagination of what isn't is the extension of a real knowledge of what is, the knowledge of a consummate observer who took no notes, except of names and dates: "If a thing didn't stay in my memory I argued it was hardly worth writing out." Knowing what the peoples, animals, plants, weathers of the world look like, sound like, smell like, was Kipling's métier, and so was knowing the words that could make someone else know. You can argue about the judgment he makes of something, but the thing is there. When as a child you first begin to read, what attracts you to a book is illustrations and conversations, and what scares you away is "long descriptions." In Kipling illustration and conversation and description (not long description; read, even the longest of his descriptions is short) have merged into a "toothsome amalgam" which the child reads with a grown-up's ease, and the grown-up with a child's wonder. Often Kipling writes with such grace and command, such a combination of experienced mastery and congenital inspiration, that we repeat with Goethe: "Seeing someone accomplishing arduous things with ease gives us an impression of witnessing the impossible." Sometimes the arduous thing Kipling is accomplishing seems to us a queer, even an absurd thing for anyone to wish to accomplish. But don't we have to learn to consent to this, with Kipling as with other good writers?—to consent to the fact that good writers just don't have good sense; that they are going to write it their way, not ours; that they are never going to have the objective, impersonal rightness they should have, but only the subjective, personal wrongness from which we derived the idea of the rightness. The first thing we notice about *War and Peace* and *Madame Bovary* and *Remembrance of Things Past* is how wonderful they are; the second thing we notice is how much they have wrong with them. They are not at all the perfect work of art we want—so perhaps Ruskin was right when he said that the person who wants perfection knows nothing about art.

Kipling says about a lion cub he and his family had on the Cape: "He dozed on the stoep, I noticed, due north and south, looking with slow eyes up the length of Africa"; this, like several thousand such sentences, makes you take for granted the truth of his "I made my own experiments in the weights, colors, perfumes, and attributes of words in relation to other words, either as read aloud so that they may hold the ear, or, scattered over the page, draw the eye." His words range from gaudy effectiveness to perfection; he is a professional magician but, also, a magician. He says about stories: "A tale from which pieces have been raked out is like a fire that has been poked. One does not know that the operation has been performed, but everyone feels the effect." (He even tells you how best to rake out the pieces: with a brush and Chinese ink you grind yourself.) He is a kind of Liszt— so isn't it just empty bravura, then? Is Liszt's? Sometimes; but sometimes bravura is surprisingly full, sometimes virtuosos are surprisingly plain: to boil a potato perfectly takes a chef home from the restaurant for the day.

Kipling was just such a potato boiler: a professional knower of professionals, a great trapeze artist, cabinetmaker, prestidigitator, with all the unnumbered details of others' guilds, crafts, mysteries, techniques at the tip of his fingers—or, at least, at the tip of his tongue. The first sentences he could remember saying as a child had been haltingly translated into English "from the vernacular" (that magical essential phrase for the reader of Kipling!), and just as children feel that it is they and not the grown-ups who see the truth, so Kipling felt about many things that it is the speakers of the vernacular and not the sahibs who tell the truth; that there are many truths that, to be told at all, take the vernacular. From childhood on he learned— to excess or obsession, even—the vernaculars of earth, the worlds inside the world, the many species into which place and language and work divide man. From the species which the division of labor produces it is only a step to the animal species which evolutionary specialization produces, so that Kipling finds it easy to write stories about animals; from the vernaculars or dialects or cants which place or profession produces (Kipling's slogan is, almost, "The cant *is* the man") it is only a step to those which time itself produces, so that Kipling finds it easy to write stories about all the different provinces of the past, or the future (in "As Easy as A.B.C."), or Eternity (if his queer institutional stories of the bureaucracies of Heaven and Hell are located there). Kipling was no Citizen of the World, but like the Wandering Jew he had lived in many places and known many peoples, an uncomfortable stranger repeating to himself the comforts of earth, all its immemorial contradictory ways of being at home.

Goethe, very winningly, wanted to have put on his grave a sentence saying that he had never been a member of any guild, and was an amateur until the day he died. Kipling could have said, "I never saw the guild I wasn't a member of," and was a professional from the day he first said to his ayah, in the vernacular—not being a professional myself, I don't know what it was he said, but it was the sort of thing a man would say who, from the day he was sixteen till the day he was twenty-three, was always—"luxury of which I dream still!"—shaved by his servant before he woke up in the morning.

This fact of his life, I've noticed, always makes hearers give a little shiver; but it is all the mornings when no one shaved Kipling before Kipling woke up, because Kipling had never been to sleep, that make me shiver. "Such night-wakings" were "laid upon me through my life," Kipling writes, and tells you in magical advertising prose how lucky the wind before dawn always was for him. You and I should have such luck! Kipling was a professional, but a professional possessed by both the Daemon he tells you about, who writes some of the stories for him, and the demons he doesn't tell you about, who write some others. Nowadays we've learned to call part of the unconscious *it* or *id;* Kipling had not, but he called this Personal Demon of his *it.* (When he told his father that *Kim* was finished his father asked: "Did *it* stop, or you?" Kipling "told him that it was It.") "When your Daemon is in charge," Kipling writes, "do not try to think consciously, Drift, wait and obey." He was sure of the books in which "my Daemon was with me . . . When those books were finished they said so themselves with, almost, the water-hammer click of a tap turned off." (Yeats said that a poem finishes itself with a click like a closing box.) Kipling speaks of the "doom of the makers": when their Daemon is missing they are no better than anybody else; but when he is there, and they put down what he dictates, "the work he gives shall continue, whether in earnest or jest." Kipling even "learned to distinguish between the peremptory motions of my Daemon, and the 'carry-over' of induced electricity, which comes of what you might call mere 'frictional' writing." We always tend to distrust geniuses about genius, as if what they say didn't arouse much empathy in us, or as if we were waiting till some more reliable source of information came along; still, isn't what Kipling writes a colored version of part of the plain truth?—there is plenty of supporting evidence. But it is interesting to me to see how thoroughly Kipling manages to avoid any subjective guilt, fallible human responsibility, so that he can say about anything in his stories either: "Entirely conscious and correct, objectively established, independently corroborated, the experts have testified, the professionals agree, it is the consensus of the authorities at the Club," or else: "I had nothing to do with it. I know nothing about it. *It* did it. The Daemon did it all." The reader of Kipling—this reader at least—hates to give all the credit to the Professional or to the Daemon; perhaps the demons had something to do with it too. Let us talk about the demons.

One writer says that we only notice what hurts us—that if you went through the world without hurting anyone, nobody would even know you had been alive. This is quite false, but true, too: if you put it in terms of the derivation of the Principle of Reality from the primary Principle of Pleasure, it does not even sound shocking. But perhaps we only notice a sentence if it sounds shocking—so let me say grotesquely: Kipling was someone who had spent six years in a concentration camp as a child; he never got over it. As a very young man he spent seven years in an India that confirmed his belief in concentration camps; he never got over this either.

As everybody remembers, one of Goya's worst engravings has underneath it: *I saw it*. Some of Kipling has underneath: *It is there*. Since the world is a necessary agreement that it isn't there, the world answered: *It isn't*, and told Kipling what a wonderful imagination he had. Part of the time Kipling answered stubbornly: *I've been there* (*I am there* would have been even truer), and part of the time he showed the world what a wonderful imagination he had. Say *Fairy tales!* enough to a writer and he will write you fairy tales. But to our *Are you telling me the truth or are you reassuring yourself?*—we ask it often of any writer, but particularly often of Kipling—he sometimes can say truthfully: *Reassuring you;* we and Kipling have interests in common. Kipling knew that "every nation, like every individual, walks in a vain show— else it could not live with itself"; Kipling knew people's capacity not to see: "through all this shifting, shouting brotheldom the pious British householder and his family bored their way back from the theaters, eyes-front and fixed, as though not seeing." But he himself had seen, and so believed in, the City of Dreadful Night, and the imperturbable or delirious or dying men who ran the city; this City outside was the duplicate of the City inside; and when the people of Victorian Europe didn't believe in any of it, except as you believe in a ghost story, he knew that this was only because they didn't *know*—he knew. So he was obsessed by—wrote about, dreamed about, and stayed awake so as not to dream about—many concentration camps, of the soul as well as of the body; many tortures, hauntings, hallucinations, deliria, diseases, nightmares, practical jokes, revenges, monsters, insanities, neu- roses, abysses, forlorn hopes, last chances, extremities of every kind; these and their sweet opposites. He feels the convalescent's gratitude for mere existence, that the world is what the world was: how blue the day is, to the eye that has been blinded! Kipling praises the cessation of pain and its more blessed accession, when the body's anguish blots out for a little "Life's grinning face . . . the trusty Worm that dieth not, the steadfast Fire also." He praises man's old uses, home and all the ways of home: its Father and Mother, there to run to if you could only wake; and praises all our dreams of waking, our fantasies of return or revenge or insensate endurance. He praises the words he has memorized, that man has made from the silence; the senses that cancel each other out, that man has made from the sense- lessness; the worlds man has made from the world; but he praises and reproduces the sheer charm of—few writers are so purely charming!—the world that does not need to have anything done to it, that is simply there around us as we are there in it. He knows the joy of finding exactly the right words for what there are no words for; the satisfactions of sentimentality and brutality and love too, the "exquisite tenderness" that began in cruelty. But in the end he thanks God most for the small drugs that last—is grateful that He has not laid on us "the yoke of too long Fear and Wonder," but has given us Habit and Work: so that his Seraphs waiting at the Gate praise God

> Not for any miracle of easy Loaves and Fishes
> But for doing, 'gainst our will, work against our wishes,
> Such as finding food to fill daily emptied dishes

praise him

> Not for Prophecies or Powers, Visions, Gifts, or Graces
> But the unregardful hours that grind us in our places
> With the burden on our backs, the weather in our faces.

"Give me the first six years of a child's life and you can have the rest" are the first words of *Something of Myself*, Kipling's reticent and revealing autobiography. The sentence exactly fits and exactly doesn't fit. For the first six years of his life the child lived in Paradise, the inordinately loved and reasonably spoiled son of the best of parents; after that he lived in the Hell in which the best of parents put him, and paid to have him kept: in " a dark land, and a darker room full of cold, in one wall of which a white woman made naked fire . . . a woman who took in children whose parents were in India." The child did not see his parents again for the next six years. He accepted the Hell as "eternally established. . . . I had never heard of Hell, so I was introduced to it in all its terrors. . . . I was regularly beaten. . . . I have known a certain amount of bullying, but this was calculated torture— religious as well as scientific. . . . Deprivation from reading was added to my punishments. . . . I was well beaten and sent to school through the streets of Southsea with the placard 'Liar' between my shoulders. . . . Some sort of nervous breakdown followed, for I imagined I saw shadows and things that were not there, and they worried me more than the Woman. . . . A man came down to see me as to my eyes and reported that I was half-blind. This, too, was supposed to be 'showing-off,' and I was segregated from my sister—another punishment—as a sort of moral leper."

At the end of the six years the best of parents came back for their leper ("She told me afterwards that when she first came up to my room to kiss me good-night, I flung up an arm to guard off the cuff that I had been trained to expect"), and for the rest of their lives they continued to be the best and most loving of parents, blamed by Kipling for nothing, adored by Kipling for everything: "I think I can truthfully say that those two made up for me the only public for whom then I had any regard whatever till their deaths, in my forty-fifth year."

My *best of parents* cannot help sounding ironic, yet I do not mean it as irony. From the father's bas-reliefs for *Kim* to the mother's "There's no Mother in Poetry, my dear," when the son got angry at her criticism of his poems—from beginning to end they are bewitching; you cannot read about them without wanting to live with them; they were the best of parents. It is *this* that made Kipling what he was: if they had been the worst of parents, even fairly bad parents, even ordinary parents, it would all have made sense, Kipling himself could have made sense out of it. As it was, his world had been torn in two and he himself torn in two: for under the part of him that extenuated everything, blamed for nothing, there was certainly a part that extenuated nothing, blamed for everything—a part whose existence he never admitted, most especially not to himself. He says about some of the things that happened to him during those six years: "In the long run these things and many more of the like drained me of any capacity for real, personal hatred for the rest of my life." To admit from the unconscious something inadmissible, one can simply deny it, bring it up into the light with a *No*; Kipling has done so here—the capacity for real, personal hatred, real, personal revenge, summary fictional justice, is plain throughout Kipling's work. Listen to him tell how he first began to write. He has just been told about Dante: "I bought a fat, American-cloth-bound notebook and set to work on an *Inferno*, into which I put, under appropriate tortures, all my friends and most of the masters." (Why only *most?* Two were spared, one for the Father and one for the Mother.) Succinct and reticent as *Something of Myself* is, it has room for half a dozen scenes in which the helpless Kipling is remorselessly, systematically, comprehensively humiliated before the inhabitants of his universe. At school, for instance: "H—— then told me off before my delighted companions in his best style, which was acid and contumelious. He wound up with a few general remarks about dying as a 'scurrilous journalist' . . . The tone, matter, and setting of his discourse were as brutal as they were meant to be—brutal as the necessary wrench on the curb that fetches up a too-flippant colt." Oh, necessary, entirely necessary, we do but torture in education! one murmurs to these methodical justifications of brutality as methodical, one of authority's necessary stages. Here is another master: "Under him I came to feel that words could be used as weapons, for he did me the honor to talk at me plentifully. . . . One learns more from a good scholar in a rage than from a score of lucid and laborious drudges; and to be made the butt of one's companions in full form is no bad preparation for later experiences. I think this 'approach' is now discouraged for fear of hurting the soul of youth, but in essence it is no more than rattling tins or firing squibs under a colt's nose. I remember nothing save satisfaction or envy when C——broke his precious ointments over my head." Nothing? Better for Kipling if he had remembered—not remembering gets rid of nothing. Yet who knows? he may even have felt—known that he felt— "nothing save satisfaction and envy," the envying satisfaction of identification. As he says, he was learning from a master to use words as weapons, but he had already learned from his life a more difficult lesson: to know that, no matter how the sick heart and raw being rebel, it is all for the best; in the past there were the best of masters and in the future there will be the best of masters, if only we can wait out, bear out, the brutal present—the incomprehensible present that someday we shall comprehend as a lesson.

The scene changes from England to India, school to Club, but the action—passion, rather—is the same: "As I entered the long, shabby dining-room where we all sat at one table, everybody hissed. I was innocent enough to ask: 'What's the joke? Who are they hissing?' 'You,' said the man at my side. 'Your damn rag has ratted over the Bill.' It is not pleasant to sit still when one is twenty while all your universe hisses you." One expects next a sentence about how customary and salutary hissing is for colts, but for once it doesn't come; and when Kipling's syntax suffers as it does in this sentence, he is remembering something that truly is not pleasant. He even manages somewhat to justify, somehow to justify, his six years in Hell: the devils' inquisitions, after all, "made me give attention to the lies I soon found it necessary to tell; and this, I presume, is the foundation of literary effort. . . . Nor was my life an unsuitable preparation for my future, in that it demanded constant wariness, the habit of observation and attendance on moods and tempers; the noting of discrepancies between speech and action; a certain reserve of demeanor; and automatic suspicion of sudden favors." I have seen writers called God's spies, but Kipling makes it sound as if they were just spies—or spies on God. If only he could have blamed God—his Gods—a little consciously, forgiven them a little unconsciously! could have felt that someone, sometimes, doesn't *mean* something to happen! But inside, and inside stories, everything is meant.

After you have read Kipling's fifty or seventy-five best stories you realize that few men have written this many stories of this much merit, and that very few have written more and better stories. Chekhov and Turgenev are two who immediately come to mind; and when I think of their stories I cannot help thinking of what seems to me the greatest lack in Kipling's. I don't know exactly what to call it: a lack of dispassionate moral understanding, perhaps—of the ability both to understand things and to understand that there is nothing to do about them. (In a story, after all, there is always something you *can* do, something that a part of you is always trying to make you do.) Kipling is a passionate moralist, with a detailed and occasionally profound knowledge of part of things; but his moral spectrum has shifted, so that he can see far down into the infrared, but is blind for some frequencies normal eyes are sensitive to. His morality is the one-sided, desperately protective, sometimes vindictive morality of someone who has been for some time the occupant of one of God's concentration camps, and has had to spend the rest of his life justifying or explaining out of existence what he cannot forget. Kipling tries so hard to celebrate and justify true authority, the work and habit and wisdom of the world, because he feels so bitterly the abyss of pain and insanity that they overlie, and can do—even will do—nothing to prevent.

Kipling's morality is the morality of someone who has to prove that God is not responsible for part of the world, and that the Devil is. If Father and Mother were not to blame for anything, yet what did happen to you could happen to you—if God is good, and yet the concentration camps exist— then there has to be *someone* to blame, and to punish too, some real, personal source of the world's evil. (He finishes "At the End of the Passage" by having someone quote: "There may be Heaven, there must be Hell. / Meanwhile there is our life here. Well?" In most of his stories he sees to it that our life here is Heaven and Hell.) But in this world, often, there is nothing to praise but no one to blame, and Kipling can bear to admit this in only a few of his stories. He writes about one source of things in his childhood: "And somehow or other I came across a tale about a lion-hunter in South Africa who fell among lions who were all Freemasons, and with them entered into a con- spiracy against some wicked baboons. I think that, too, lay dormant until the Jungle Books began to be born." In Chekhov or Turgenev, somehow or other, the lions aren't really Freemasons and the baboons aren't really wicked. In Chekhov and Turgenev, in fact, most of the story has disappeared from the story: there was a lion-hunter in South Africa, and first he shot the lions, and then he shot the baboons, and finally he shot himself; and yet it wasn't *wicked*, exactly, but human—very human.

Kipling had learned too well and too soon that, in William James's words: "The normal process of life contains moments as bad as any of those which insane melancholy is filled with, moments in which radical evil gets its innings and takes its solid turn. The lunatic's visions of horror are all drawn from the material of daily fact. Our civilization is founded on the shambles, and each individual existence goes out in a lonely spasm of helpless agony. If you protest, my friend, wait till you arrive there yourself!" Kipling had arrived there early and returned there often. One thinks sadly of how deeply congenial to this torturing obsessive knowledge of Kipling's the First World War was: the death and anguish of Europe produced some of his best and most terrible stories, and the death of his own son, his own anguish, produced "Mary Postgate," that nightmarish, most human and most real daydream of personal revenge. The world *was* Hell and India underneath, after all; and he could say to the Victorian, Edwardian Europeans who had thought it all just part of his style: "You wouldn't believe me!"

Svidrigailov says: "We are always thinking of eternity as an idea that cannot be understood, something immense. But why must it be? What if, instead of all this, you suddenly find just a little room there, something like a village bath-house, grimy, and spiders in every corner, and that's all eternity is. . . . I, you know, would certainly have made it so deliberately." Part of Kipling would have replied to this with something denunciatory and biblical, but another part would have blurted eagerly, like somebody out of *Kim*: "Oah yess, that is dam-well likely! Like a dak-bungalow, you know." It is an idea that would have occurred to him, down to the last *deliberately*.

But still another part of Kipling would suddenly have seen—he might even later have written it down, according to the dictates of his Daemon—a story about a boy who is abandoned in a little room, grimy, with spiders in every corner, and after a while the spiders come a little nearer, and a little nearer, and one of them is Father Spider, and one of them is Mother Spider, and the boy is their Baby Spider. To Kipling the world was a dark forest full of families: so that when your father and mother leave you in the forest to die, the wolves that come to eat you are always Father Wolf and Mother Wolf, your real father and real mother, and you are—as not even the little wolves ever quite are—their real son. The family romance, the two families of the Hero, have so predominant a place in no other writer. Kipling never said a word or thought a thought against his parents, "both so entirely comprehending that except in trivial matters we had hardly need of words"; few writers have made authority so tender, beautiful, and final—have had us miserable mortals serve better masters; *but* Kipling's Daemon kept bringing Kipling's stories in which wild animals turn out to be the abandoned Mowgli's real father and mother, a heathen Lama turns out to be the orphaned Kim's real father—and Kipling wrote down the stories and read them aloud to his father and mother.

This is all very absurd, all very pathetic? Oh yes, that's very likely; but, reader, down in the darkness where the wishes sleep, snuggled together like bats, you and I are Baby Spider too. If you think *this* absurd you should read Tolstoy—all of Tolstoy. But I should remark, now, on something that any reader of Kipling will notice: that though he can seem extraordinarily penetrating or intelligent—inspired, even—he can also seem very foolish or very blind. This is a characteristic of the immortals from which only we mortals are free. They oversay everything. It is only ordinary readers and writers who have ordinary common sense, who are able to feel about things what an ordinarily sensible man should. To another age, of course, our ordinary common sense will seem very very common and ordinary, but not sense, exactly: sense never lasts for long; instead of having created our own personal daydream or nightmare, as the immortals do, we merely have consented to the general daydream or nightmare which our age accepted as

ANGUS WILSON

Kim *and the Stories*

It is [his] Indian vision that Kipling will surely above all be remembered by, for the British Indian scene (native and Anglo-Indian) is a composition of relationships that no one else has ever put on paper, and no one else has ever made into a consistent social metaphor for human existence. A very strange man expressed himself here through a very strange, now historical, phenomenon. Against this, the obvious imperfections of the young Kipling's mind and the crudities of his craftsmanship in the early stories seem of little importance. The brashness, the assumed man-of-the-world voice, the club gossip, the know-all "I" narrator, the occasional puritan's leer, the arch biblical pastiche language and the even more arch forays into pseudo-Arabian Nights narration—all these are minor flaws in a great East Window that shines and glints and darkens and dazzles as nothing else in any literature. There are some truly inferior stories among the scores of his Indian tales and more mediocre ones, and enough masterpieces—but the vision should be taken as a whole from the first tale, "Lispeth" in *Plain Tales from the Hills* to her reappearance in *Kim*—should be taken good and bad alike, with *Departmental Ditties* and *Barrack-Room Ballads* thrown in. One must be grateful to Andrew Rutherford, for example, for making a selection of Kipling's later stories for the two Penguin volumes (though I do not always agree with his choice), but the Indian work must stand as it is, in all its imperfections and its glories. . . . Kipling's India speaks for itself. The *Jungle Books*, I think, need a short explanation, for they are very odd. And, of course, *Kim*, his

From *The Strange Ride of Rudyard Kipling*. © 1977 by Angus Wilson. Viking, 1978.

most magical work, one of the oddest masterpieces ever written, demands our full scrutiny.

Three of the seven stories in *The First Jungle Book* and five out of the eight in *The Second Jungle Book* concern Mowgli and his jungle empire. For many people Mowgli, Baloo, Bagheera, Kaa and Co. *are* the *Jungle Books*— a kind of Greyfriars. But the merits of the individual Mowgli stories vary very much. Only a few, and perhaps only parts of these, show Kipling at his very top form.

The interest in the Mowgli group as a whole cannot really be a literary one. It is connected with his pervasive idea of the Law which is expressed in them more continuously than in the rest of his work, although hardly less obscurely. But first I should mention the two or three non-Mowgli stories whose excellence has been overshadowed by that attractive jungle predecessor of Kim.

"Rikki Tikki Tavi" has rightly commanded some attention because the fight between the mongoose and the snakes takes place in that clearly seen backyard bungalow compound which is Kipling's visual forte; but is marred surely for modern readers by the whimsical intrusion of the human family.

"The Miracle of the Purun Bhagat" is a very fine story. It tells of the Indian Minister who rises to be the toast of London's smart dinner tables and to win the K.C.I.E. and who then changes overnight to become a wandering Sunyassi or holy man. It has been hailed as Kipling's tribute both to educated India and to the Hindu way of life. And so it is both; but it has also been pointed out that the dénouement of the story, when the holy man, up in the foothills of the Himalayas, leaves his anchorite's rock cell to warn villagers of an impending avalanche, is a tribute to the western code of action rather than to the Hindu way of passivity. This is surely right, but it is also no chance mistake of Kipling's. He is attempting to pay tribute to both systems and yet to suggest that the western creed of human concern will assert itself in a crisis.

Whether he is right or not, the story convinces. It is surely a curtain raiser to *Kim*, in which the Lama's Wheel and the Great Game (East and West) meet in one man, Purun Bhagat.

Apart from its excellence as a story, the most curious feature of "The Miracle of Purun Bhagat," to me, is how Kipling's verbal picture of the Hindu holy man talking with the beasts in his cell, brings to mind some stained glass picture of St Francis and the birds, as it might have been painted by his Uncle Ned Burne-Jones. It is perhaps just a little too delicately beautiful to stand beside Kipling's other tributes to the Indian natural scene where the fierce roughness of life always shows through. Is this perhaps why he incorporated a story of such adult concern in a book on the surface intended for "juveniles"?

"The Undertakers," the story of the riverbank predators—the mugger-crocodile, the jackal, the adjutant stork—is unique in his work, for, in the hypocritical dialogue between these three ruthless cowards he creates a wonderful interchange, humorous and stylised, that might come out of Ben Jonson's *Volpone* or *The Alchemist*.

Yet the accent, for all their unevenness, must fall upon the Mowgli group. In the first place, these stories make the most central statement about the Law, that ill-defined, yet absolute and categorical barrier that stands between man and anarchy, and, more importantly, between man and the probably meaningless death and destruction that await him and all his works.

This concept of the Pervasive Law that must rule all human action, with its accompanying doctrine of stoic social duty to back it up; its alleviation of that stoicism by means of Stalkyish cunning and tricks that mock a too solemn or too slavish interpretation of the Law's Dictates and by means also of group loyalties, more or less mystic (Freemasonry, Mithraism, clubs, regiments, professions, crafts—above all, families), has necessarily attracted the attention of sociologists. For it goes plain against the historical optimistic progressive strain that usually informed all English social thought in Kipling's day, derived from Locke and Bentham. Lord Annan has interestingly shown how close Kipling's approach is to Continental social philosophy of the time. But I agree with Mr Sandison in thinking that Lord Annan, in his intentness upon this different aspect of Kipling's thought, has placed too much emphasis on Kipling's political (in the widest sense) view of man, on society as being more important than the individual in Kipling's work. . . . The proper centre of that strange world *is* the individual, the lost, scattered individuals—unsure of their identities—"Who is Kim?"—finding temporary security before the inescapable and probably final fact of death in duty and suffering with dignity and in keeping out anarchy. As Mr Sandison says, contrary to Lord Annan's view, Kipling doesn't subordinate the individual to society, he invents a rigid social rule (the Law) to shield the individual (and himself) from a constant nagging anxiety about his ultimate fate. Indeed the whole of this book is intended to suggest that Kipling's art is suffused with a personal and mysterious despair and apprehension of exactly this kind.

Where I do not agree with Mr Sandison is in his condemnation of Kipling's violent hostility to those—frivolous like the Bandar-log monkeys, brutally unlawful like Shere Khan the tiger; or cunningly parasitical like the jackal—who seek to evade the Law, to demand more for the individual than Kipling's grim role. For Mr Sandison, this is a central defect in Kipling, a dog-in-the-manger hostility to those who have tried to seek more personal fulfilment, perhaps more pure pleasure. Part of this, it is true, is due to Kipling's innate puritanism that makes him hostile to hedonism. It is often disagreeable. The superior beauty of *Kim* or of some of the Mowgli tales or of Purun Bhagat's tale (the three are linked in many ways) comes from the absence of this constant apprehensive condemnation of those who do not accept the restraints that Kipling's own anxiety places upon the human race. But then, in varying degrees, these three works try to fuse the real world with the Garden of Eden, Kipling's dream world of childhood. Yet, in the main body of his work where the individualists and pleasure seekers are fiercely condemned as frivolous, dangerous, overweening or a source of corruption, it is not, I think, as Mr Sandison would suggest, from any grudge of Kipling's against those who try to get more out of life (and sometimes succeed in so doing) than he does. It is an essential part of his anxious, doom-threatened world that man should take on his duty, even if it be, as in "The Children of the Zodiac," Leo's duty of singing his poems to the people to alleviate their lot for the little time left them before Death closes in, should follow the Law for other men's sake and his own so that they can forget the probable oblivion ahead in the orderly exercise of a patterned life. The condemnation, then, of the Bandar-log, and the Black Rat at the Mill Dam, and Aurelian McGoggin, and the Wax Moth, and the Mugger, and Shere Khan, and Jellaludin McIntosh is not just for their selfishness and frivolity but because they will bring horror to themselves and other men if their anarchic behaviour spreads. But finally, I am not sure, interesting though these speculations about the Law are, whether they throw so much light on the excellencies of Kipling's work, upon the way he creates his magical effects. With Shamsul Islam, I would say that Kipling was neither a thinker nor a sociologist but primarily an artist.

The chief glory of his art in the Mowgli stories lies in his extraordinary combination of the natural and animal world with the world of the humans. Baloo is a bear and a housemaster; Bagheera is chiefly a leopard but a wise, sensual man more worldly than the bear; Kaa is primarily a python, delighting in his coils and glistening skin, lusting to chase and kill, but he is also an exceptional and clever man, knowing himself yet accepting the Law, perhaps a true intellectual as opposed to the Bandar-log who are monkeys and "intellectuals"; the jackal is Mussolini's forerunner, and Shere Khan Hitler's, as wartime telegrams between the Kipling Society and General Wavell rightly suggested.

It is a strange achievement, a brilliant artistic bluff, where words and thoughts veer towards the human and movements, vision and feeling are as near to animal as a writer can hope to guess. And, of course, the whole is made credible by the extraordinary evocation of the jungle itself (which perhaps Kipling had only seen in the photographs that the Hills brought back from Seonee) and the powerful effect that Chitor's ruins had upon him. The Law in this world is exact but far from Darwinian; we need note only that no animal will attack another at the pool in time of drought.

Into this world comes the lovable, strong, highly intelligent wolf-cub boy, Mowgli, who learns the simple Law which in more complicated form he will have later to follow in human society. And, by his superior human intelligence and compassion, eventually also wins mastery in the animal world. The Law of the jungle is absolute and can be followed by the animals with comparative ease, for they do not know tears or laughter, the things that make man's life both more glorious and more complex and far more painfully burdensome among human beings than has ever been known in the Eden of Kaa and Baloo, however bloody and terrible many of the deeds that happen in the jungle.

All this about the Law is interesting, but as far as Kipling's art goes, it often gets in the way, with too much didactic moralising. In *The First Jungle Book*, only one story is reasonably free from it and that doesn't really get going until halfway through. "Kaa's Hunting" contains one of the most horrible scenes in all Kipling's work—and that work contains many such. It is the picture of the Bandar Log monkeys swaying helplessly towards their doom in the great ruins of the King's palace in a hypnotic trance induced by the coiling and looping of Kaa, the python's body and his "never stopping, low humming song." It is made more terrible by the jungle fact that, were it not for Mowgli's human unsusceptibility to the snake's enchantment, Baloo and Bagheera, Kaa's erstwhile cohunters, would inevitably sway towards their death with the monkeys. For, in the jungle, all alliances—and bear, python and leopard have hunted together to rescue Mowgli—break up when the kill is on. It is made, indeed, even a little too horrible by a certain relish with which Kipling recites the awful fate of the frivolous, mischievous monkey folk.

The best Mowgli stories come in *The Second Jungle Book*. The manoeuvres by which Mowgli lures the ravening hordes of dholes, the red dogs from the South, to their death and the battle between the dholes and the wolves is one of the best action narratives in fiction.

The crown of the two books is "The King's Ankus," Kipling's best use of myth in all his work. The story opens deceptively and purposely as the most sensually idyllic of all the scenes in this Eden, with Mowgli "sitting in the circle of Kaa's great coils, fingering the flaked and broken old skin that lay looped and twisted among the rocks just as Kaa had left it. . . . It is very beautiful to see—like the mottling in the mouth of a lily." This lolling in the python's folds during the heat of the day gives way to the evening visit to the jungle pool. "Then the regular evening game began—of course Kaa could have crushed a dozen Mowglis if he had let himself go. . . . They would rock to and fro . . . till the beautiful, statue-like group melted in a whirl of black and yellow coils and struggling legs and arms." But the jungle paradise of learning life's laws and strengthening the body is always circumscribed by what event the wisest of the animal-preceptors, even Kaa, the python, doesn't understand; such unknown dangers nearly always relate to men and their ways.

So it is in "The King's Ankus." Mowgli, sleepy and relaxed after his wrestling, expresses his content: " 'What more can I wish? I have the Jungle and the favour of the Jungle. Is there anything more between sunrise and sunset?' " It is then that Kaa, who loves the boy, as all his animal protectors do, pours into Mowgli's ear (serpent-like) the knowledge of something new. A very old white cobra, that lives deep beneath the ruins of Cold Lairs, guards a mass of objects (Kaa could make neither head nor tail of them) that have been in his care for centuries—they are, the old cobra says, things "for the least of which very many men would die." Mowgli is sure that these new things "*must* be a new game," but Kaa declares, "it is *not* game. It is—it is—I cannot say what it is." It is, of course, the treasure of the kings who once ruled in the ruined city, gold and jewels in abundance, described by Kipling in a restrained *Yellow Book* manner that is as pleasing as it is fitting.

The white cobra is one of Kipling's most fascinating creatures. In it he suggests that sense of something repulsive and frightening that, if we are honest, we must admit to find in some very old people. His situation is immediately pathetic to us—an old lost creature, faithful to his duty, not understanding that the world above is not still a wonder city of kings and palaces and royal elephants, not knowing that the jungle has taken over. But the cruelty, the venom that lies beneath the pathos soon shows itself, as he seeks to entrance Mowgli with the treasure, as all humans are entranced by gold, and then to make sport, in killing the trapped boy. "Is this not worth dying to behold? Have I not done thee a great favour?" he asks, and then calls to the angry Kaa, "See the boy run. There is room for great sport here. Life is good. Run to and fro awhile and make sport, boy." But the cobra is impotent as well as old, his venom has dried up. Mowgli scorns to kill him, as he also scorns the royal jewels and coins he does not understand. His curiosity only bids him take the jewelled and golden ankus or royal elephant yoke. And in a day, he sees four men lose their lives in lust for it. At last, he takes it back into the cobra's deep den. he is not yet ready to leave his jungle Eden, perhaps the sight of what gold does to men has even deferred his instinctive urge to grow towards manhood by a story or two.

But at last it comes in "The Spring Running," where Bagheera the leopard, seeing the boy in tears, says that he will soon leave the jungle for human life, for animals don't know tears. This final story is a moving, if a little disjointed piece. Mowgli goes off to assume later his proper human duty under the Law as a member of the Forestry Service of the Indian Government of Her Majesty (told in "In the Rukh," a story published earlier than the *Jungle Books*). But, in fact, Mowgli, the wolf boy in the jungle, is surely only the shadowy if delightful precursor of Kim, the street arab, who knows all guiles yet remains in Eden innocence, a far more delightful hero, for, unlike Mowgli, his zest for life is not the product of bodily health and physical content only, but of an endless desire to see and know new things. Kipling takes his myth of Eden away from the world of animals, where Mowgli is the master of the Jungle, to the scene of the Grand Trunk Road so rich in human variety, where Kim is something much better than a master—the Little Friend of all the World.

It is rare to find readers, Kipling fans or others, who are not captivated by *Kim;* it is equally rare to find many who can offer any detailed account of their enjoyment of the book. "Oh! *Kim*, of course, is a magical book," is the usual general account that follows a detailed discussion of his other works. And so it is. I shall try here to account for its magic.

Kipling's mention of it in *Something of Myself* is at once proud and slightly dismissive, as though he were not quite sure how to account for the extraordinary thing he had made. Indeed, I wonder if he did realise quite how strange a masterpiece he had produced during those eight years or so. *Kim* had first inspired his imagination in the early days of his married life in Vermont, that halcyon time when Josephine was the summit of his delight— a young baby that was his own. The novel had continued to fire his fancy through all the bitter sweets of the failure of his American dream, and on beyond the nightmare of Josephine's untimely death in New York. At last he had finished it at his parents' retirement home in Tisbury, happily recalling the Lahore family times, his father advising on Buddhism, his mother teasing him on his failure to invent a plot.

It was the longest time that he took to write any book. It was said to subsume the unwritten novel, *Mother Maturin*, that Lockwood disapproved of; and this alone can excuse Lockwood's interference. It has a deeper connection with great fictions of the past than any other of his work. He himself was aware of the picaresque connection with Cervantes—surely because the

Lama and his chela, Kim, are so happy a recall of Quixote and Sancho Panza, a deeper, more original recall than Pickwick and Sam Weller. He succeeds overall in something that Dickens dared to attempt, that no writer, I think, has tried. For in Kim himself, he unites the knowingness, the cunning, the humour and the appeal of the Dodger, with the gentleness and goodness of Oliver Twist, a seemingly impossible task. And I think that the scenes where Lurgan, the antique dealer of Simla, instructs Kim and the Hindu boy in various memory games and competitions in disguises to prepare them for espionage work must have been written with at least some half-memory of Fagin's instruction of Oliver and the boys in thieving. As to the rich and various Indian life of the Grand Trunk Road which is so vital a part of Kim's pleasure in novelty and variety, it owes something, I think, on its didactic side to Kipling's loved *Pilgrim's Progress;* but the didactic side of *Kim* is always played down—one of the reasons for the book's greatness—and the Grand Trunk Road owes more to another of Kipling's favourite works—Chaucer's *Canterbury Tales.* But I name these impinging masterpieces of the past not to suggest any derivative quality in *Kim,* for it is its absolute originality that is its making, but rather to suggest the sort of literary heights in which we are travelling in this strange work.

The most striking feature of *Kim* is sounded early on, when we are told that Kim "did nothing with an immense success." "He lived in a life as wild as that of the Arabian Nights, but missionaries and secretaries of charitable societies could not see the beauty of it. His nickname through the wards was 'Little Friend of all the World' . . . he had known all evil since he could speak—but what he loved was the game for its own sake." His two small companions playing on the gun outside the Lahore Museum are a Moslem boy and a Hindu, "Chota Lal . . . His father was worth perhaps half a million sterling, but India is the only democratic land in the world." Kim's superiority to them both is at once declared when the strange figure of the Tibetan Lama appears on the scene, for Chota Lal is afraid of him and the Moslem boy despises him as an idolator, but Kim is immediately drawn to him—he is new.

And his love of the new, this thirst for fresh experience and changing scenes persists in Kim's young life: on the Grand Trunk Road, "there were people and new sights at every stride—castes he knew and castes that were altogether out of his experience"; and with the important Sahiba's entourage (the Wife of Bath's world) "this was the life as he would have it—bustling and shouting, the beating of bullocks and the creaking of wheels, lighting of fires and cooking of food, and new sights at every turn of the approving eye. . . . India was awake and Kim was in the middle of it." Colonel Creighton, who sees Kim as good material for the Spy Service, knows at once how to attract him: "In three days thou wilt go with me to Lucknow, seeing and hearing new things all the while." When Kim sleeps among Mahbub Ali's horses and unwashed men we are told, "change of scene, service and surroundings were the breath of his little nostrils."

I know of no other English novel that so celebrates the human urban scene (for English novelists are all touched by the romantic country worship) except for that utterly dissimilar book *Mrs. Dalloway;* and when one reads of Kim's thoughts, "this adventure, though he did not know the English word, was a stupendous lark," one is reminded of the opening passage of Virginia Woolf's novel (Clarissa's thoughts as she steps out into the streets of London): "What a lark! What a plunge!" It is a note of delight in life, of openness to people and things that is maintained throughout the novel and is the essence of its magic.

Kipling's passionate interest in people and their vocabularies and their crafts is, of course, the essence of the magic of all his work. But in all the other books it tends to be marred by aspects of his social ethic—by caution, reserve, distrust, mastered emotion, stiff upper lips, direct puritanism or the occasional puritan's leer, retributive consequences, cruelty masquerading as justifiable restraint or bullying as the assertion of superiority. None of these is present in *Kim*.

Kipling's social ethic, it is true, is there in Kim's apprenticeship to "the Game," the British Secret Service in India. This is the way that, as a sahib's son, he will serve the British cause. This has stuck in the gullet of many liberal critics, notably Edmund Wilson. But I think that fine critic and lovable man was misled by his strong dislike for British imperialism.

True, Kim will be serving British rule, but this must be read within the context of Kipling's belief that the two higher values in the book—the richness and variety of Indian life and the divine and spiritual idiocy of the Lama—can only be preserved from destruction by anarchic chaos or from despotic tyranny by that rule. This is directly underlined in the scene when Kim bears the letter to Creighton from Mahbub Ali that tells of the plotted rising in the North. The Lama, thinking of how far he has come from his monastery, laments, "Alas! it is a great and terrible world!" And Kipling immediately writes, "Kim stole out and away, as unremarkable a figure as ever carried his own and a few score thousand other folks' fates around his neck." In short, the Lama in his spiritual revulsion from the world, innocently does not know the real and terrible dangers that threaten the ordered society in which he can safely seek his sacred river; but Kim, by his involvement in the Game, can help to preserve that holy man whose spirituality he can glimpse and love but never hope to achieve. And let us note, it is a game, however terrible a one, in which Kim, by his strange street-arab status of friend of all the world and night climber across rooftops, is peculiarly associated—a game in which he must be able to carry maps in his head and remember a hundred objects seen and be able to pass disguised as twenty or so other people. These powers make him perfect material for a spy; the same powers made Kipling a great writer of fiction.

But, if the moralising side of Kipling is only lightly present in *Kim*, implicit in the Game, the corruption of Kim's world is always implicit rather than stated. The world Kim moves in is no ideal one. Only the Lama in his innocence mistakes the generous prostitute for a nun. It is a world of lies— Kim knows the Lama for a rarity because he tells the truth to strangers. Physical danger is constant and real. Human life is not held in high regard— Mahbub Ali is prepared to sacrifice Kim's life to get his message to Creighton, yet he loves Kim strongly and jealously. Few of the fifty or so vividly realised characters are without his or her faults, but most are made generous and loving by contact with Kim and the Lama. Yet Kim is never above the ordinary dishonesties and tricks of daily life. As the Lama says, "I have known many men in my long life, and disciples not a few. But to none among men, if so be thou art woman-born, has my heart gone out as it has to thee—thoughtful, wise and courteous; but something of a small imp."

And it is not Kim's virtues alone that win him the friendship of all the world. He is remarkably physically beautiful and, in a way that is successfully kept by Kipling from being fully sexual, flirtatious with all and sundry. It is part of his worldly guile. The prostitute in the train is won over by him as is the other prostitute who dresses him up when he escapes from St Xavier's School; the Sahiba's motherliness has an earthy tinge; the woman of Shamlegh yearns for him. In Lurgan's shop, as I have said, the jealousy of the Hindu boy has obvious sexual overtones; as I think does the jealousy of the horse dealer, Mahbub Ali, for Kim's overriding devotion to the Lama. Yet all this sensuality is without an explicit sexual tinge. I do not believe that this is Victorian self-censorship upon the part of Kipling. It is certainly not an avoidance of the subject in a book ostensibly intended for the young, for the scene where a prostitute tries to steal from Mahbub Ali is quite explicit. It is, I think, one more aspect of the purposeful attempt by Kipling in this novel to create a world that is real and ideal at one and the same time. Nor is the absence of overt sex offensively evasive as a modern critic might think; it is just a natural part of the innocent-corrupt world in which Kim lives.

As to evil, it is strikingly absent, as may be measured by the unimportance of the "villains," the Russian and French spies. They are bad men, we know, or they offer violence to a very good man, the Lama. But their retribution is not the savoured brutal one of so many of Kipling's stories. They merely pass out of the novel, mocked by all the Himalayan villagers as they make off with their tails between their legs. Their humiliation is like that of Trinculo and Stephano on Prospero's magic island in *The Tempest* and we bless the babu Hurree Singh, who mocks them, as we bless Ariel. In default of true evil, we must judge the English chaplain, Bennett, as the villain, for he lacks all concern for freedom and variety, virtues so surprisingly celebrated by Kipling in this book. It could be said that this absence of real evil prevents *Kim* from vying with the great novels of the past as a "mature" book; but, in compensation, it must surely be said that this creation of an innocent world of guile makes it an unequalled novel.

Nirad Chaudhuri has said that *Kim* is the very best picture of India by an English author; and I am sure he is right. But rich and convincing though the varied Indian characters are, and splendid though the evocations of the Indian scenes are from the Jain Temple outside Benares to the Himalayan foothills, it is yet Kipling's own India as Kim is Kipling's own street-arab and the Lama Kipling's own Buddhist. Many Indian critics, notably K. Jamiluddin in *The Tropic Sun*, have pointed out that Buddhism is a very strange choice of religion to represent India, from which it has been absent for centuries. No doubt, Kipling was a bit influenced in his choice by his desire to draw on his father's special knowledge; but I think he was even more concerned to pose his own version of self-abnegation against his own version of commitment to the world as represented by Kim. The Lama and Kim make a most delectable Prospero and Ariel. And it is no sparring partnership for either, since the Lama's greatest erring from the Way is in his attachment to his Chela, and Kim comes close to exhausting his adolescent physical strength in bringing his master down from the mountains. The story of Kim and the Lama is, in the last resort, beneath all its superbly realised human and topical detail, an allegory of that seldom portrayed ideal, the world in the service of spiritual goodness, and, even less usual, spiritual goodness recognising its debt to the world's protection. It is the culmination and essence of all the transcendence that Kipling gained from his Indian experience. In it alone of all his works he does ask, "Who is Kim?" although he cannot answer the question. In a sense, his answer is the book itself, for it is the best thing he ever wrote.

IRVING HOWE

The Pleasures of Kim

That sense of evil which for cultivated people has become a mark of wisdom
and source of pride, indeed, the very sun of their sunless world, is not a
frequent presence in the pages of *Kim*, and when it does appear it can rarely
trouble us with either its violence or grasp. We are inclined these days to
exalt the awareness of evil into a kind of appreciation. We find it hard to
suppose that a serious writer could turn his back upon the malignity at the
heart of things; we urge it as a criticism of writers like Emerson and Whitman
that they are weak in the awareness of evil, as if nature had denied them a
necessary faculty. But *Kim* is unsubdued by the malignity at the heart of
things. Whatever evil it does encompass tends to be passed off onto a troop
of bumbling Russian spies who muddle along on the northern borders of
India, stage-comic Russians about as alarming as Laurel and Hardy. *Kim* is
at ease with the world, that unregenerate place which is the only one most
of us know, and because at ease, it can allow itself to slide toward another
possible world, one that some of us may yet come to know. For readers
trained in the severities of Kafka and Sartre, all this may constitute a literary
scandal, especially if one goes so far as to make a claim for the seriousness
and greatness of the book; and precisely this scandal is what I propose here
to cultivate.

There is greater scandal. *Kim* evokes and keeps returning to sensations
of pleasure, a pleasure regarded as easy, natural, and merited. Our sophistication teaches us that all the literary works we esteem can be expected to

From *Art, Politics, and Will: Essays in Honor of Lionel Trilling,* edited by Quentin
Anderson, Stephen Donadio, and Steven Marcus. © 1977 by Basic Books, Inc.

yield pleasure; that the torments, dryness, and even boredom of certain exemplary twentieth-century texts can also be made to yield pleasure. Our sophistication muddies the issue. For the pleasure of *Kim* is of a more traditional and unproblematic sort, a pleasure in the apprehension of things as they are, in embracing a world as enchanting as it is flawed. Kipling's book accepts the world's body, undeterred by odors, bulges, wrinkles, scars. Life, in its final bearing, may prove to be absurd, but *Kim*, though far from an innocent book, has little commerce with this view, since it is a book that takes delight in each step of the journey bringing us closer to the absurd: delight in our clamor, our foolishness, our vanity, our senses, and—through the lumbering radiance of the lama who comes from and goes back to the hills of Tibet—delight in an ultimate joy of being which beckons from the other side of sensuous pleasure but which, implies Kipling, those of us not lamas would be advised to seek through pleasure.

Part of the pleasure that *Kim* engages is that of accepting, even venerating sainthood, without at all proposing to surrender the world, or even worldliness, to saints. *Kim* embraces both worlds, that of the boy and the lama, the senses and beyond, recognizing that anyone who would keep a foot, or even a finger, in both of these worlds must have some discipline in adjustment and poise—otherwise, what need would there be for the lama's or any other serious education? But never for a moment does the book propose to smudge the difference between the senses and beyond, or worse still, to contrive some facile synthesis. The "Wheel of Things," to which we are all bound in this world, and the "Search," by which we may penetrate another, have each their claim and dignity. The two speed along in parallel, but what they signify cannot readily be merged. There is earth, there is spirit, both are real. In any case, a writer open to the allurements of pleasure is more likely to explore the Many than strain toward the One.

And greater scandal still: *Kim* is the work of a man quite unable to evoke the admiration we give to culture heroes. He is a jingo and a bully, or defender of bullies; he swaggers in the style of an overgrown schoolboy; he is usually more talented than wise. That there was a "wound behind his bow" hardly excuses all that we find unattractive in Kipling: there is a wound behind every bow. He is not a writer we take to heart, as one takes Hardy, or respect unreservedly, as one respects Chekhov. Yet this often small-spirited writer composed, once in his life, a book of the most exquisite radiance of spirit, breathing a love of creation such as few of his greater contemporaries could match. There is a puzzle here, and I propose to let it remain.

The story starts with noises of sociality. Kim is a thirteen-year-old darling of the streets, a fast-talking urchin, white by birth and dark from the sun, who awaits each day as an encounter with possibility. Trading amiable epithets with the bazaar merchants who call him "Little Friend of all the World," Kim is neither innocent nor naive. He has "known all evil since he could speak," but he does not let it determine or overwhelm him; he absorbs and then puts aside that knowledge, as if breaking a skin, for there is always something to see and experience in the streets of Lahore, that "wonderful walled city." In these streets he is as shrewd as his distant cousin Huck Finn is shrewd along the shore; like that cousin, he has learned "to avoid missionaries and white men of serious aspect," and also has learned the fine art of doing "nothing with an immense success." Whenever he sidles up to a booth, the men of the city smile, knowing they will hear something clever or mischievous and will enjoy his command of the Indian art of cursing. He is a young entrepreneur and apprentice con man, a quick-change artist who does not care for any fixed or even steadily emergent self because life offers so many selves to discover and try out. "Who is Kim?" he will ask himself later in the book, and each chapter will yield the happy answer that there are many answers. He loves "the game for its own sake"—the "game" standing here for both the British Secret Service, with which he will become enmeshed through his worldly self, and the entirety of the business of life. "The game" is not an adequate term, or concept, at all; it reflects the all-too-familiar side of Kipling's sensibility which is adolescent and stunted.

When Kim meets the lama, an ungainly rhapsodist who makes transcendence seem a familiar option, the two of them quickly find common ground. They share a meal, they bound their territory, they match prospects for the future. To the boy, the old man represents a new experience, a guru such as the mainland does not yield; for the old man, the boy is a guide through the bewilderments of India and a friend ripening into a *chela* or disciple. Kim is possessed by the evidence of his senses, the lama with a vision beyond, and the book will make as its central matter an unfolding of the love between the two, that thrill of friendship which in nineteenth-century literature comes to replace the grace of God.

At first Kim literally takes the old man in hand. He goes to beg food for him, charmingly vain in the confidence with which he can tap the city. "They ate together in great content"—so begin and end half the great stories of mankind. Awakened after a sleep brought on by the meal, the old man looks for the boy and is bewildered to find Kim in one of his transmutations, "a Hindu urchin in a dirty turban." One thinks to compare this moment with the trick Huck plays on Jim, but only to reject the comparison, since everything is far gentler in Kipling's India than in Twain's America, and

Kim need not go through torments of conscience in order to declare himself "thy chela," certainly need not declare himself ready, like Huck, for perdition. Because he is utterly fortified in his sense of being at home in the world and feels some mild superiority to the unworldliness of the old man, Kim can also begin to see, in an incipient way, that the lama represents other possibilities for him: " 'I have never seen anyone like to thee in all this my life. I go with thee.' " It is not yet a spiritual discipleship; it is simply a companionship of the road. "Boy-like, if an acquaintance had a scheme, Kim was quite ready with one of his own." Perhaps, he smiles to himself, "they will make me a king" during the journey. To which the lama replies: " 'I will teach thee other and better desires upon the road.' "

But not yet, not at the beginning. The first five chapters of the book form a picaresque entry into "the great good-tempered world," first on the "te-rain" and then along the Great Trunk Road (India's Mississippi). It is an India refracted through Kipling's adoring memory and in its relation to the "real" India complex beyond hope of disentangling. It is an India Kipling loves for its rough vivacity, its easy mixture of manners, its encompassing of gutter and cloud; and it is praised by him (as if to unsettle all those who declare settled views of his work) as the "only democratic land in the world"— by which he means, I gather, not the absence of rank or distinction but a readiness to live with and intermingle all ranks and distinctions. (At this point historical fact and imaginative vision may find themselves at considerable odds: a problem by no means confined to Kipling, indeed, common to all serious novelists.) In Kipling's India—Kim's playground—the boy is a trickster delighting in his tricks and expecting that his audiences will delight with him in seeing, and seeing through, them. A people raised with a sense of hazard appreciates the boy's virtuosity; shrewdly eyes his performance, an utterly this-worldly performance; yet looks tolerantly upon "holy men stammering gospels in strange tongues." The multiplicity of visions and ways that Kipling attributes to India becomes the ground of his delight.

Kim and the lama now move through a world that is like a vast, disorderly bazaar., People are quick to embrace and to anger. They speak suddenly from the heart, as if any traveler may be a friend. They curse with the expertness of centuries. ("Father of all the daughters of shame and husband of ten thousand virtueless ones, thy mother was devoted to a devil, being led thereto by her mother.") Their ripeness shows itself in a linked incapacity to be surprised and readiness to enjoy the familiar. Running errands for Mahbub Ali, the free-thinking Afghan horse trader who initiates him into the British Secret Service, Kim charms a fierce-tongued old Indian lady (straight in the line of Chaucer, from one pilgrimage to another) into helping him and the lama. He trades stories with retired soldiers, jests with travelers, even pokes a little tender fun at his lama—for this is Kim's world, a stage for his multiple roles as urchin, beggar, raconteur, flirt, apprentice spy, and apprentice *chela*, who is always eager, as Kipling shrewdly notes, for "the visible effect of action." Picked up by some British soldiers who propose to educate him ("sivilize," says Huck), Kim tells the lama: "Remember, I can change swiftly." It is the motto of every youth trying to evade the clamp of civilization.

And the world's evil? The poverty, injustice, caste rigidities which must have been so grinding in the India of eighty years ago? If it would be morally shameful to suppress these questions entirely, it would also be foolish to let them deprive us of the pleasures of *Kim*.

There is a "literary" way of coping with these questions, but like all merely "literary" ways, it seems to me finally unsatisfying. Kipling's book releases a distinct, which is necessarily to say, a limited vision. It seeks to give life a desirable look; it brushes past social misery as more recent novels brush past personal happiness; it neglects the shadows as others neglect the lights; it sees the world as fresh, alluring, and young—young, in India! But *Kim* is not an idyll, not a retreat from the world; it is a celebration of, a plunge into the world.

Let us try another tack. The book has no assured answers to the questions of Indian poverty, injustice, and caste rigidity, partly because it does not choose to give them priority, though we surely know that it is not an evasive or willfully "positive" book. All the wrongs and evils of India are there, steeped in the life of the people, yet these do not keep them from grasping the sensations of their moment, or from experiencing the appetites and ceremonies they rightly take to be their due. What so wonderfully distinguishes Kipling's characters is their capacity for shifting from treble to bass, from pure spirit to gross earth, from "the Search" to "the Game." It is as if their culture actually enables them to hold two ideas in their heads at once. The India of Kipling is a place in which people live by custom and caprice, fixed in ways given them yet ready to move past those ways when they feel a need to. They make life for themselves, and it has its substance.

One great flaw in the reforming passion, as Ralph Ellison reminded me during a polemic about black fiction a decade ago, is that in its eagerness to remedy social wrongs it tends to neglect the experience, certainly to undervalue the experience, of those whose lives it wishes to improve. It does not weigh or honor fully enough the life-hungers, the life-capacities of the oppressed. Now Kipling, it is true, did not see India as particularly oppressed, and I am as ready as the next liberal or radical to deplore this failure; but he did see the people of India as vigorous, full of humor and energy, deeply worthy. How are we to explain that in the pages of this apologist for imperialism, the masses of India seem more alive, more autonomous than in the pages of writers claiming political correctness?

Regarding Kipling's apparent indifference to the social evils of India there remains another and more radical "answer." Though in much of his work he shows a quite sufficient awareness of evil, even at some points an obsessive concern, he seems really to want to persuade us through *Kim*, his most serious book, that in the freshness of a boy's discoveries and the penetration of an old man's vision, evil can become ultimately insignificant, almost as nothing before the unsubdued elation of existence, almost as nothing before the idea of moral beauty. Others in the West and the East, long before Kipling, have said as much, though few have embodied it with the plastic vividness that Kipling has. I will confess here to not entirely grasping the import of this vision of ultimate goodness or harmony; I find it a kind of moral slope, very slippery, very attractive. Yet in reading *Kim* one may yield to this vision, just as one might for a moment come to accept beatitude upon meeting a saint. Nor should we try to get round the problem by remarking that *Kim* is a children's book. For it seems intolerable that the best things in life should be supposed available only to children. Old bones have their rights too.

The middle portion of *Kim*, another five chapters, brings to an end the rapturous picaresque of boy and old man: it must come to an end. Kim is sent to the white man's school, to be trained as the son of a *sahib* that he is; he will be prepared for the "Great Game," the world of power, rationality, governance. Who is Kim, he now asks himself with an anxiety that is new to him. "He considered his own identity, a thing he had never done before, till his head swam." He submits to the disadvantages of the whites, though he is still persuaded in his heart that he is one of the blacks—" 'when the *madrissah* [school] is shut, then I must be free and go among my people.' " On vacations he "changes swiftly," drops his European being, dresses as an Indian, returns to "my people." The lama fades out of the picture, while still, in the style of a Dickens's benefactor, supporting Kim in the white man's school. "Come to me! Come to me! Come to me!" the boy writes to him in an outburst of longing, and when they meet for a short while it is now in open love. " 'If I eat thy bread,' cried Kim passionately, 'how shall I ever forget thee?' " The old man consoles him: " 'Do not weep; for look you, all Desire is illusion, and a new binding upon the Wheel. Go up to the Gates of Learning. Let me see thee go. . . . Doest thou love me? Then go, or my heart cracks.' " The boy goes, to learn his trade, to be tested by other agents, British and Indian, to become part of the Game, a man who can govern.

These chapters are beautifully done, with delicacy in shifting from milieu to milieu, but they are minor Kipling rather than major: the adventures here are more like those of Tom Sawyer than those of Huck Finn. And they leave us somewhat uneasy. Edmund Wilson, who thought *Kim* "almost a first-rate book," put his finger on the source of this uneasiness: "What the reader tends to expect is that Kim will come eventually to realize that he is delivering into bondage to the British invaders those whom he has always considered his own people, and that a struggle between allegiances will result. . . . We have been shown two entirely different worlds existing side by side, with neither really understanding the other, and we have watched the oscillations of Kim, as he passes to and fro between them. But the parallel lines never meet; the alternating attractions felt by Kim never give rise to a genuine struggle."

About Wilson's criticism Noel Annan remarks:

> No doubt this is what a courageous liberal writing at a time when Gandhi and Congress were struggling for Indian independence did expect, but such a conflict is imposed by the critic on the novel. No doubt the future life of a young agent would have entailed confounding Indian resistance to the British, but this is an *ex post facto* judgment, and in the novel such a career is depicted as the maintenance of that minimum of order such as is necessary to prevent foreign intrigue, frontier invasions, and injustices by native princes and to permit the joyous, noisy, pullulating mess of Indian life on the Great Trunk Road to continue.

Annan's reply is adequate as far as it goes, but we might try to go a little farther. And oddly, it is Wilson who, in the very course of his complaint, provides our answer. "The parallel lines [between what the lama signifies and what the English require] never meet; the alternating attractions felt by Kim never give rise to a genuine struggle." Precisely so; indeed, that is Kipling's major theme—the parallel lines *cannot* meet. For what impinges upon Kim's consciousness are not two systems of political beliefs, or social orders, but two ways of apprehending human existence, each of which is shown to have its own irreducible claims. The dualism that Wilson deplores yet keenly notices lies at the very heart of the book.

Would it, in any case, make much difference if Kim were to join an incipient Indian nationalist movement instead of the British Secret Service? Would he still not have to undergo a similar training in the ways of the

world, a similar apprenticeship in stratagems and devices? Would he still
not be torn between the irreconcilable claims of this world and another?
Would not the lama still remain before him as a loving apparition of a "Way"
never to be accepted wholly but never to be abandoned wholly?

Most of us, I suppose, would be happier if Kim worked for a Gandhi
or some forerunner of Gandhi rather than Colonel Creighton, the head of
the British Secret Service, since that would ease our discomfort with the
part of Kipling which, intellectually, we find insupportable. But for the
dynamic of the novel itself, for the inner development of Kim, it would not
matter decisively. The Secret Service, rather than a secret underground, is
what Kipling's experience made available to him at a fairly superficial plane
of consciousness; it is a given of the world in which he grew up, the India
of his youth, and it is not, one notes with gratitude, subjected to any quick
"purification" by virtue of Kim's service to the lama. All that the Game—
the Secret Service and its prep-school hijinks—need really do is to embody
the Wheel of Things, that terrestrial "illusion" which the first portion of the
book has shown to be the substance of delight.

The parallel lines of the two main actions draw closer and closer in the
concluding chapters, a soaring movement of ecstasy, one of the most beautiful
set-pieces in the English language. It is Kipling's skill, but behind that skill,
his easiness and poise as a juggler of worlds, which leads him to see that the
two lines of action can indeed by brought very close together but that their
meanings, their "ways" must remain beyond conciliation.

Kim's mission for the British service leads him toward Tibet, in a
pleasantly exciting rigmarole about chasing off Russian spies; his mission as
the lama's *chela* leads him toward Tibet, where the old man, as a mighty
walker of the hills, takes on a new energy, but also sins through his lapse
into anger when he is struck by one of the Russians. Everything comes finally
into place, even that coarse-grained love for the world which the lama, here
if nowhere else, finds himself sharing:

> "These are the hills of my delight! Shadows blessed above all
> other shadows! There my eyes opened on this world; there my
> eyes were opened to this world; there I found Enlightenment;
> and there I girt my loins for my Search. Out of the Hills I came—
> the high Hills and the strong winds. Oh, just is the Wheel." He
> blessed them in detail—the great glaciers, the naked rocks, the
> piled moraines and tumbled shale; dry, upland, hidden salt-lake,
> age-old timber and fruitful water-shot valley one after the other,
> as a dying man blesses his folk, and Kim marvelled at his passion.

Both Kim and the lama suffer brief, sharp moments of crisis: the boy, his mission successful, is diverted into helping the old man and succumbs to a kind of breakdown of uncertainty, while the old man, though believing himself at the verge of nirvana, forces himself to return to this world out of his love for the boy:

> Then a voice cried: "What shall come to the boy if thou art dead?"
> and I was shaken back and forth in myself with pity for thee;
> and I said: "I will return to my *chela* lest he miss the Way." Upon
> this my Soul . . . withdrew itself from the Great Soul with striv-
> ings and yearnings and retchings and agonies not to be told. . . .
> I pushed aside world upon world for thy sake.

It is a climax of rhapsodic union, but only of the boy and the old man, not the two Ways. One of Kipling's best critics, J. M. S. Tompkins, notices that "the beauty of *Kim* lies largely in the figure of the lama. . . . Benign, courteous, humble and clean of heart, but a man of authority in his place and time, he draws Kim not to any mystical height—the boy remains firmly terrestrial and takes a very practical view of the lama's immersion in the River of the Arrow—but to a perception of these qualities in his master."

All through the last third of the book there run a series of anticipatory communions, moments of meeting between the two, in which all seems at peace in, and out of, the world. As they eat together, Kim recognizes: " 'And we are beyond all castes.' " The old man speaks "as a Seeker walking in humility, as an old man, wise and temperate, illumining knowledge . . . till Kim, who had loved him without reason, now loved him for fifty good reasons." And "each long, perfect day rose behind Kim for a barrier to cut him off from his race and his mother-tongue."

There are moments of pure charm: " 'These,' " says the lama, " 'are indeed my Hills. Thus should a man abide, perched above the world, sep-arated from delights, considering vast matters.' " And Kim answers: " 'Yes, if he has a *chela* to prepare tea for him, and to fold a blanket for his head, and to chase out calving cows.' " There are moments of pure yielding, when they wearily make their way down from the hills, the lama weakens, and Kim "held the weary head on his lap through the noonday heats." The lama cannot help remarking how strange it is that a young sahib should serve him so, and Kim replies: " 'Thou hast said there is neither black nor white. Why plague me with this talk, Holy One? Let me rub the other foot. It vexes me. I am not a Sahib, I am thy *chela*, and my head is heavy on my shoulders.' "

For all that *Kim* can be seen (not very profitably, I think) to strike a contrast between East and West, Buddhism and Christianity, it is far more harmonious and accepting, far more "organic," than *Huckleberry Finn*, the book to which it bears so many surface similarities. In Twain's story there is hardly a profitable, let alone pleasurable entry into the world; there can only be an escape from it, for a moment or two, on a floating raft. Nothing along the shores of the Mississippi seems as rich or refreshing as the mundane world into which Kim and the lama plunge at the outset of their journey, and finally Twain's book comes to be a much more otherworldly, much more despairing book than *Kim*, even though, or perhaps because, it has no lama, no religious atmosphere, no invocation of the Great Soul. For Kim, while yielding himself to the lama, also feels "with an almost audible click . . . the wheels of his being lock up anew on the world without. Things that rode meaningless on the eyeball of an instant before slid into proper proportion. Roads were meant to be walked upon, houses to be lived in, cattle to be driven, fields to be tilled, and men and women to be talked to."

The parallel lines, then, move endlessly into the future, without joining or reconcilement. Yet a mark of transfiguration has been stamped upon the book; whatever he may do, Kim will forever and beyond forgetting be the old man's *chela*. That mark of transfiguration is of course the print of love, and one can only wonder, in putting down this incomparable book, how strongly Kipling was aware that in guiding his two friends through pleasure and into the joy of being, he may also have been leaving pleasure behind.

DONALD DAVIE

A Puritan's Empire: The Case of Kipling

In an unconsidered moment—or rather in one very ill-considered under-taking, *After Strange Gods*, a book that he was later ashamed of—T. S. Eliot spoke of the Congregationalism that D. H. Lawrence grew up in as "vague hymn-singing pietism." It was an aberration that F. R. Leavis never allowed Eliot, nor the rest of us, to forget about. Years later it may be thought that Eliot more than made up for it, when he wrote appreciatively of another English author, one who stands in almost exactly the same relation to Wes-leyan New Dissent that Lawrence stood in to Old Dissent. This author was Rudyard Kipling, grandson to Wesleyan ministers on both sides of his family, but whose parents conformed to nonpracticing Anglicanism, and who was himself some sort of undogmatic theist. Of Kipling Eliot wrote in 1941:

> He might almost be called the first citizen of India. And his relation to India determines that about him which is the most important thing about a man, his religious attitude. It is an at-titude of comprehensive tolerance. He is not an unbeliever—on the contrary, he can accept all faiths: that of the Moslem, that of the Hindu, that of the Buddhist, Parsee or Jain, even (through the historical imagination) that of Mithra: if his understanding of Christianity is less affectionate, that is due to his Anglo-Saxon background—and no doubt he saw enough in India of clergy such as Mr. Bennett in *Kim*.

This is liberal indeed and represents (it may be thought) a great increase in

From *The Sewanee Review* 87, no. 1 (Winter 1979). © 1979 by Donald Davie.

Christian charity over the Eliot who wrote *After Strange Gods*, the Eliot to whom his Anglican allegiance was so much more of a recent and exciting novelty.

However, before we set this change of heart entirely to Eliot's credit, we need to take note of certain difficulties which arise in our reading of the poet for whom he is soliciting our admiration. There is for instance what is probably the most justly famous of all Kipling's poems, his "Recessional" of 1897, quoted in part here:

> God of our fathers, known of old,
>> Lord of our far-flung battle-line,
> Beneath whose awful Hand we hold
>> Dominion over palm and pine—
> Lord God of Hosts, be with us yet,
> Lest we forget—lest we forget!
>
> . . . .
>
> If, drunk with sight of power, we loose
>> Wild tongues that have not Thee in awe,
> Such boastings as the Gentiles use,
>> Or lesser breeds without the Law—
> Lord God of Hosts, be with us yet,
> Lest we forget—lest we forget!

The line in this poem that has set most teeth on edge and raised most blood pressures is the notorious one about "lesser breeds without the Law"—a line which has been frequently misunderstood, for the good reason that the intended sense of it—by which the "lesser breeds" are not brown Afghans but white Germans—is so far from obvious. What has given less trouble, though I find it much more troublesome, is the question: *What* god of *whose* fathers? *What* lord of *whose* battle-line? The god of the German (or Russian, or Dutch Boer) battle-line is officially the Christian God, who is also— officially—the god of Mulvaney and Ortheris and Learoyd, of Tommy Atkins, "the absent-minded beggar ordered south." And so it can hardly be He to whom "Recessional" is addressed. Nor can we any more plausibly identify Him as Allah or Siva or Buddha or Mithras or the god of the Parsee or the god of the Jain; although, since Kipling is fervently aware of the Indian regiments fighting beside the British in Burma and South Africa, it might reasonably seem that the God addressed should incorporate these unchristian deities at the same time that it excludes the Christian deity of Imperial Germany. How can we know where we stand, with a poem addressed to a Being so ambiguous? And yet Eliot, the devout and proudly orthodox Anglo-

Catholic author of *Four Quartets,* knew just where *he* stood in respect of the poem, and where the poem stood in relation to him: "I call Kipling a great hymn writer on the strength of *Recessional.* It is a poem almost too well known to need to have the reader's attention called to it, except to point out that it is one of the poems in which something breaks through from a deeper level than that of the mind of the conscious observer of political and social affairs— something which has the true prophetic inspiration. Kipling might have been one of the most notable of hymn writers." This is liberal theology indeed! The Eliot whose polemics ever since "For Lancelot Andrewes" had insisted on the necessity for religious *dogma* here shows himself ready to admire a hymn that has "prophetic inspiration," though that inspiration is unleashed in the service of a Divinity undefined and undefinable. This more than makes up for Eliot's sneer at Lawrence's Congregationalism, in the sense that it overcompensates, flies to the other extreme.

Eliot had not taken leave of his senses, however. The "Lord God of Hosts" of "Recessional" can indeed by identified, by just that phrase and by others in the poem that support it, particularly "Such boastings as the Gentiles use." The God addressed in "Recessional" is the God of the Old Testament, God of Israel, God of "the chosen people." If we needed sup- porting evidence—as in fact we don't—that evidence is in Kipling's poem of a year before, "Hymn before Action," which Eliot does not fail to include in his *A Choice of Kipling's Verse* immediately before "Recessional":

> The earth is full of anger,
>   The seas are dark with wrath,
> The Nations in their harness
>   Go up against our path:
> Ere yet we loose the legions—
>   Ere yet we draw the blade,
> Jehovah of the Thunders,
>   Lord God of Battles, aid!

The God invoked in "Recessional," it now appears, is not the God of Christ any more than He is the God of the Jain or the Parsee: He is the God of David, warrior king of ancient Israel.

Yet what right has Kipling, or Eliot after him, to appeal to this god, this *Yahwe?* Was Kipling, any more than Eliot, to convert to Judaism from Christianity? Quite evidently not, and so the charge of culpable frivolity lies as heavily as ever against the pair of them.

Here we may leave Eliot, remarking compassionately that in 1941 there was much excuse for a naturalized Englishman—a patriot as only the naturalized can be—to nourish the patriotic will at the expense of intellectual confusion. For Kipling there can be no such excuse. And the further we probe into Kipling's religious sentiments the more confusion we find—and the less excuse for it.

In the 1920s his cousin Stanley Baldwin, recording how in a conversation with Kipling he had found them at one on political matters, accounted for this by saying: "We have common puritan blood." What Baldwin seems to have had in mind was that their common great-grandfather, the Scottish Ulsterman James Macdonald, had been a Wesleyan minister converted by the great John Wesley himself. We need not deny that evangelical Wesleyanism was historically an offshoot of English puritanism. But it was a very peculiar offshoot, one that ranged itself against such great dissenting puritans as Oliver Cromwell and John Bunyan, with both of whom Kipling nonetheless aligned himself under the illusion (apparently) that in doing so he was keeping faith with his Wesleyan inheritance. Historically Wesleyanism was High Church, aggressively royalist, Arminian, and Tory. Accordingly, if Kipling had really thought through his inheritance of Wesleyan puritanism—and *Puck of Pook's Hill* is there to show how he thought such "thinking through" was a patriotic duty—he ought to have sided with the Arminian Archbishop Laud against the Calvinist Cromwell, and with the nonjuring Arminian William Law against the Calvinist Bunyan. The Arminian conviction that Christ died for *all* men, not just for the elect, was crucial for Kipling, since it was the only basis on which for instance Gunga Din might earn salvation; and in any case the torments he suffered from his South Sea foster mother in boyhood seem to have derived from her being an evangelical Calvinist. Yet "Recessional" depends, if it is not to fall apart completely, on the Calvinist notion of a chosen people, the elect. In short, if Kipling shared his cousin Baldwin's conviction that they shared a "puritan" inheritance—and there is every reason to think that he did—he seems to have been wholly ignorant of the mutually irreconcilable strains inside English puritanism. The two logically incompatible theories of salvation, Arminian and Calvinist, are in "Recessional" held together by a powerfully traditional rhetoric; but the slightest attention to what that hymn seems to say will reveal the two incompatible systems and will break the poem in two.

Eliot decided that Kipling "can be called a Tory in a sense in which only a handful of writers together with a number of mostly inarticulate, obscure and uninfluential people are ever Tories in one generation." This enabled Eliot to clear Kipling, and also incidentally Eliot himself, from the imputation, common in 1941 and still common in England today, that the true Tory of this recondite sort is in any way friendly to fascism—the truth being instead, as Eliot says finely, that fascism, "from a truly Tory point of view, is merely the extreme degradation of democracy." Kipling certainly deserved to be rescued from this imputation, if only because of his excellent poem "The Storm Cone," in which as early as 1932 he warned against the Nazis. But as Eliot remarked further, in any less recondite sense of "Tory," anything having to do with the alignment of political parties at Westminster, Kipling was not a Tory at all. On the contrary it was the Tory party under Balfour that he assailed, savagely and bravely, in "The Islanders" (1902), with its famous and blistering indictment of "the flannelled fools at the wicket or the muddied oafs at the goals." And I think we can go further, so far as to say that Kipling believed in what has since been labeled the Whig interpretation of English history. For nothing else seems to explain his lifelong admiration of Cromwell, so much at odds with his Wesleyan inheritance and his Arminian predilections. What a strain it was for him to accommodate his Cromwellianism in the frame of his other commitments appears most strikingly from a poem that Eliot chose not to reprint, "The Old Issue," dated October 9, 1899, the date of President Kruger's ultimatum which precipitated the Boer War:

> All we have of freedom, all we use or know—
> This our fathers bought for us long and long ago.
>
> Ancient Right unnoticed as the breath we draw—
> Leave to live by no man's leave, underneath the Law.
>
> Lance and torch and tumult, steel and grey-goose wing
> Wrenched it, inch and ell and all, slowly from the King.
>
> Till our fathers' stablished, after bloody years,
> How our King is one with us, first among his peers.
>
> So they bought us freedom—not at little cost—
> Wherefore must we watch the King, lest our gain be lost.
>
> . . . .
>
> (Time himself is witness, till the battle joins,
> Deeper strikes the rottenness in the people's loins.)
>
> Give no heed to bondsmen masking war with peace.
> Suffer not the old King here or overseas.
>
> They that beg us barter—wait his yielding mood—
> Pledge the years we hold in trust—pawn our brother's blood—
>
> Howso' great their clamour, whatsoe'er their claim,
> Suffer not the old King under any name!

> Here is naught unproven—here is naught to learn.
> It is written what shall fall if the King return.
>
> He shall mark our goings, question whence we came,
> Set his guards about us, as in Freedom's name.
>
> He shall take a tribute, toll of all our ware;
> He shall change our gold for arms—arms we may not bear.
>
> He shall break his Judges if they cross his word;
> He shall rule above the Law calling on the Lord.

This has been called complex. It is certainly complicated, and could hardly be anything else if it was to accomplish its strenuous and implausible purpose of persuading the forces of the queen-empress, as they advanced on the independent South African Republic, that they were in the same case as the Parliamentary armies of the 1640s advancing on the loyal armies of Charles I. The crossing over of terms in this complicated equation, so that monarchical equals parliamentarian, and republican equals despotic, is, to say the least of it, audacious. And the strenuousness of the maneuver distorts, retrospectively, the "Recessional" of two years earlier. For there the "Law" that the lesser breeds were "without" (i.e., lacking, but also "outside of") was the Law of Moses, which bore upon Israel but not on other nations; whereas in "The Old Issue" when Paul Kruger is said to "rule above the Law," the "Law" is the constitutional law of the land, and the other "Law," the Law of Moses, is presumably what the Calvinist Kruger might say he was appealing to when he was "calling on the Lord." No wonder that F. W. Reitz, secretary of state of the South African Republic, should hurl the accusation back again:

> Gods of the Jingo—Brass and Gold,
>   Lords of the world by "Right Divine,"
> Under whose baneful sway they hold
>   Dominion over "Mine and Thine."

It is certainly on the face of it more plausible to see the divine right of government, which Charles I claimed and the Cromwellians denied, being asserted by Queen Victoria than by President Kruger. Kipling has the rhetoric, but common sense and probability are all with Reitz.

It may well be thought that subsequent history has vindicated Kipling in his suspicions of the Afrikaner's mentality and his political instincts. The pro-Boer demonstrators of 1900—among them Kipling's aunt, Georgiana Burne-Jones—would be the antiapartheid demonstrators of today. And it is true that Kipling foresaw the black South Africans getting a worse deal from the Afrikaners than from the British. But it's no good pretending that the welfare of the blacks carried any weight with Kipling when he called for war with the Boers; his case, as "The Old Issue" makes clear, rested solely on the penalties imposed upon English-speaking "Uitlanders" in the Orange Free State and the Transvaal. And certainly Calvinist theocratic republics have a poor record of safeguarding civil rights, ever since Calvin's own Geneva and the seventeenth-century Commonwealth of Massachusetts. But was it not just such a theocratic republic that was created in England by Cromwell and the other regicides? And were not just as many Englishmen deprived of their rights under the regicides as under the king who had been killed? "The Old Issue" is outrageous special pleading.

Yet we need not think that Kipling was insincere when he wrote it. On the contrary we have already found reason to think that what looks like duplicity is muddle and ignorance about the nature of the English "puritan" tradition, muddle which—now as fifty years ago—is to be found particularly among those who, like Baldwin, boast of having "puritan blood." "Puritan" is not synonymous with "nonconformist," nor with "evangelical"; still less with "parliamentarian" or "democratic" or "Cromwellian." Of these adjectives the only ones that fit the Wesleyan inheritance are "evangelical" and, less certainly, "puritan"; but Kipling, I suspect, thought that all the other adjectives were appropriate also. In short I believe that Angus Wilson is right when, on the last page of his *Strange Ride of Rudyard Kipling*, after considering various psychological explanations of the riddle that Kipling's life and works present us with, he decides: "I prefer if I must a social-historical description of long generations of Evangelical belief ending in post-Darwinian doubt."

The question of Kipling's sincerity comes up again as soon as we shift our attention from the Evangelical generations behind him to the post-Darwinian doubt that he lived in. And from this point of view it is "Recessional," not "The Old Issue," that looks inexcusable. Sons who conceive themselves to have no God at all, or only a God who is nebulous and featureless, have no right to call for help in battle on the God of their fathers whose features were stern and strong. Eliot, who decided Kipling was a great hymn writer because of "Recessional," claims for him also that he was a great epigrammatist: "Good epigrams in English are very few; and the great hymn writer is very rare. Both are extremely objective types of verse: they can and should be charged with intense feeling, but it must be a feeling that can be completely shared. They are possible to a writer so impersonal as Kipling."

The force of what Eliot means to say here is carried in the words *objective* and *impersonal*. But it is not clear what he means by either of these words; and if we look elsewhere in his criticism for enlightenment, we come across the famous essay "Tradition and the Individual Talent," which advances a theory of "the impersonal" that has been generally found unacceptable. I believe he is maintaining here that in a hymn (or an epigram) a poet who doesn't believe in the God of either the Old or the New Testament can properly write as if he did so believe, because by that pretense he can share the intensity of his feeling—a feeling not religious at all, but political and patriotic—with the mass of his countrymen who either *do* believe in such gods or else think that they do. And when he cryptically quotes in full a difficult and memorable later poem, "The Fabulists," I think (for it is impossible to be sure) that he reads this poem as an impenitent confession by Kipling that he did indeed go to work in that way. However that may be, and whether or not that is a right reading of "The Fabulists," few readers will be ready to agree that, by making this play with "objective" and "impersonal," Eliot has cleared the author of "Recessional" from the charge of insincerity, of duplicity and double-dealing.

This is not to say that there is no way for an atheistic or agnostic poet, a poet of "post-Darwinian doubt," to draw on the themes and images of Christian belief. Many will agree that one of Kipling's nonbelieving contemporaries, Thomas Hardy, showed how this could be done, with moving propriety and sincerity. I need cite only "The Oxen":

> Christmas Eve, and twelve of the clock.
> "Now they are all on their knees,"
> An elder said as we sat in a flock
> By the embers in hearthside ease.
>
> We pictured the meek mild creatures where
> They dwelt in their strawy pen,
> Nor did it occur to one of us there
> To doubt they were kneeling then.
>
> So fair a fancy few would weave
> In these years! Yet, I feel,
> If someone said on Christmas Eve,
> "Come; see the oxen kneel
>
> "In the lonely barton by yonder coomb
> Our childhood used to know,"
> I should go with him in the gloom,
> Hoping it might be so.

"Hoping it might be so" expresses the agnostic sentiment with a purity, a plain and aching accuracy, such as we look for in vain anywhere in Kipling. And no talk of *objective* and *impersonal* can persuade us that "Recessional" in some quite different way is an equal or comparable achievement.

But this is not the only way in which a non-Christian or post-Christian poet can, with perfect sincerity, traffic in Christian affairs. For an alternative way of doing so we can turn to Kipling's "Gethsemane" (which, says Eliot the wily possum, "I do not think I understand"):

> The garden called Gethsemane
>   In Picardy it was,
> And there the people came to see
>   The English soldiers pass.
> We used to pass—we used to pass
>   Or halt, as it might be.
> And ship our masks in case of gas
>   Beyond Gethsemane.
>
> The garden called Gethsemane,
>   It held a pretty lass,
> But all the time she talked to me
>   I prayed my cup might pass.
> The officer sat on the chair,
>   The men lay on the grass,
> And all the time we halted there
>   I prayed my cup might pass.
>
> It didn't pass—it didn't pass—
>   It didn't pass from me.
> I drank it when we met the gas
>   Beyond Gethsemane!

This is one of Kipling's greatest poems. And Eliot understood it well enough, in the sense that he understood it to be overtly and fiercely blasphemous. The poem furiously denies what every Christian is required to believe— that one Being and one alone, Jesus, suffered on behalf of humankind an agony more intense and more expiatory than ever was, or ever would be, required of another. The Christian may be, he *must* be, shocked and affronted by this; but he cannot object to it, cannot deny that Kipling had the right to say it. Such blasphemy is thoroughly plain dealing: there is nothing devious nor duplicitous. (Poetically of course—for *poetically* is the word here, not *rhetorically*—the uncannily piercing moment comes with the officer sitting on the chair, the exquisitely painful metrical disturbance that lays a doubled trisyllabic rhythm on to the iambic norm.) Straightforward blasphemous denial is another way for the non-Christian poet to deal sincerely with Christianity. Closely related to this, and yet crucially different, is Kipling's use of scripture in two stories about the Great War, "The Madonna of the Trenches" and "The Gardener." Angus Wilson, himself I think no Christian, is quite right to protest that in both these cases the use of the scriptural text is both tasteless and redundant. In the first case, where a sergeant's suffering for an unattainable woman is identified with St. Paul's suffering for Christ, there is "plain sentimentality clothed in a metaphysical authority which it does not possess"; and in the second, better story, when the war cemetery's gardener is revealed to the Mary Magdalen figure as Christ himself, this has the surely unintended implication that no merely human compassion could have embraced her. Kipling seems to have intended to be blasphemous far more often than he succeeded in being so: this was because he had an uncertain grasp of what blasphemy is. This uncertainty didn't in the least diminish his appeal to an exceptionally wide public; for in a post-Darwinian, post-Christian or at best nominally Christian culture, people have an uncertain grasp of blasphemy to just the extent that they have an imperfect grasp of faith. Once again, in this matter of blasphemy, it seems we can acquit Kipling of duplicity and insincerity, and convict him rather of muddle—a remarkably *fruitful* muddle, because it was a muddle that he shared with his readers, and not just with readers from the educated elite that provided other writers of his time, such as Hardy, with a far more limited public than the one Kipling could appeal to.

Can this be our compassionate if contemptuous verdict on Kipling's writings as a whole? I think not. "Recessional" is still the sticking point. To see in that poem no duplicity but only confusion we have to strain every nerve and give Kipling the benefit of every doubt. Moreover in Eliot's *A Choice of Kipling's Verse* there are two more poems which, if they are set side by side, raise once again in an acute form our suspicions about Kipling's good faith. These two poems go together because they both deal with another heroic figure from the English puritan past—not Cromwell, but Bunyan. They are "The Holy War" of 1917, and "MacDonough's Song," which may have been written about 1907 though it did not appear until *A Diversity of Creatures* in 1910. "The Holy War" is distressing rant, and it is astonishing that Eliot should have chosen it for his selection:

> All enemy divisions,
>   Recruits of every class,

And highly screened positions
    For flame or poison-gas;
The craft that we call modern,
    The crimes that we call new,
John Bunyan had 'em typed and filed
    In Sixteen Eighty-two.

Likewise the Lords of Looseness
    That hamper faith and works,
The Perseverance-Doubters
    And Present-Comfort shirks,
With brittle intellectuals
    Who crack beneath a strain—

. . . .

The Pope, the swithering Neutrals,
    The Kaiser and his Gott—
Their rôles, their goals, their naked souls—
    He knew and drew the lot.

The earlier poem is much more distinguished writing, and just for that reason
it is, especially at the end (which I shall not quote), even more shocking.
But what rocks us on our heels is that Bunyan's very phrase "The Holy
War," which in 1917 is endorsed and applauded, had those several years
before been treated with searing contempt:

Whether the State can loose and bind
    In Heaven as well as on Earth:
If it be wiser to kill mankind
    Before or after the birth—
These are matters of high concern
    Where State-kept schoolmen are;
But Holy State (we have lived to learn)
    Endeth in Holy War.

(Just so; but Holy War against the Boers was precisely what Kipling had
preached in "The Old Issue"!) "MacDonough's Song" is part and parcel of
a story, "As Easy as A.B.C.," which is set in the year 2065 A.D. And so we
may say—it seems we *must* say—that Holy War will be manifestly a vicious
and desolating idea in 2065, though it is a wholesome and invigorating idea
in 1917. But this implies a relativism—about art and morals and politics,
indeed about *truth*—for which the only word is *cynical*. And if this is what

"puritanism" brings us to, as soon as it is conceived of as a secular and time-bound entity persisting apart from religious faith, then "puritan blood" is what no one can or should take pride in. One does not have to be a knee-jerk liberal, nor one of the "brittle intellectuals," to believe that the Kipling who thought this, and perverted his poetic vocation to serve this kind of thinking, is indeed in many ways the diabolical figure that many of us supposed him to be, before Eliot and George Orwell some forty years ago began to rehabilitate him.

ZOHREH T. SULLIVAN

Kipling the Nightwalker

Now that Irving Howe has made portable the voluminous voice of the hooligan Kipling (*The Portable Kipling* [New York: Penguin, 1982]), and now that he has linked Kipling's name with that of our original father Freud as a writer sharing a similar deep anxiety over discipline, authority, and the fate of civilization, perhaps Kipling will once again be read by a public that feels certain he is not worth reading. In spite of praise from his most unlikely contemporaries—from Henry James and Oscar Wilde to C. S. Lewis and T. S. Eliot—in spite of Edmund Wilson's pioneering essay on the biographical sources of his fictional anxieties ("The Kipling That Nobody Read"), in spite of splendid critical biographies by C. E. Carrington, Philip Mason, and Angus Wilson, collections of his works were never in demand, seldom reprinted, and never successful in the paperback market. Even the Signet paperback inspired by the movie *The Man Who Would Be King* lost all demand along with diminishing lines at the movie theaters. And Randall Jarrell's luminous introduction to fifty of his favorite Kipling stories (reprinted in *A Sad Heart at the Supermarket*) was done for a collection now out of print. After lamenting the common perception that "Kipling was someone people used to think was wonderful, but we know better than that now," and after comparing some of his humor and his respect for the ordinary with that of Shakespeare and Chekhov, Jarrell concludes:

> Kipling is neither a Chekhov nor a Shakespeare, but he is far
> closer to both than to the clothing-store-dummy-with-the-solar-

From *Modern Fiction Studies* 30, no. 2 (Summer 1984). © 1984 by Purdue Research Foundation.

topee we have agreed to call Kipling. Kipling, like it or not, admit it or not, was a great genius; and a great neurotic; and a great professional, one of the most skillful writers who have ever existed—one of the writers who have used English best, one of the writers who most often have made other writers exclaim, in the queer tone they used for the exclamation: "Well, I've got to admit it really is *written*."

Increasingly, critics from Edmund Wilson to Randall Jarrell, and most recently John A. McClure, have drawn attention to Kipling's psychological complexity, his sense of terrifying powerlessness and isolation in a hostile world, his fear of "a certain darkness into which the soul of the young man sometimes descends—a horror of desolation, abandonment, and realised worthlessness, which is one of the most real of the hells in which we are compelled to walk." Kipling's life project was an attempt to negotiate descents into uncontrollable elements—darkness, water, and the unconscious itself.

As a study in such psychological negotiations, Kipling's most compelling and curiously neglected story is "The Brushwood Boy." Somerset Maugham in his introduction to a few of the tales concludes that, though the dreams in "The Brushwood Boy" are fascinating, the outer story is dull, and one must finally look upon it "not as a tale that has any relation to real life, but as much of a fairy story as The Sleeping Beauty or Cinderella." And Angus Wilson in his splendid biography dismisses "The Brushwood Boy" as one of the dream stories whose "vision is flawed with whimsy or self-pity." Although it is indeed a highly charged fantasy, the story is neither whimsical nor trivial. Rather, it is Kipling's fullest, most explicit dream story that taps his most personal core of recurring fears, fantasies, and myths. What I hope to establish in this reading is that the thematic, psychological, and structural principles at work in this story resonate through Kipling's fiction and his autobiography, that the dream life of the brushwood boy mirrors not only what George Cottar represses but all Kipling journeys that take their protagonists over much threatening landscape only to teach them how *not* to immerse themselves in its destructive elements. As a significant example of a paradigmatic Kipling story, its action involves the protagonist in a descent into unconscious material that conforms to, rather than transcends, the values of his waking life. Yet, as this essay will demonstrate, in both autobiography and fiction nightwalking is a persistent theme that held special charms for Kipling. It signaled a delicate encounter with the repressed that always threatened to return, and thereby offered the protagonist yet another test and a chance for mastery over the unconscious and the uncontrollable.

On its simplest waking level, "The Brushwood Boy" is an initiation story about the typical training of a colonialist, George Cottar (the brushwood boy), from childhood to maturity. We follow his rise in the ranks and his public successes through school, Sandhurst, and India, after which he returns to his parental home in England to receive his final reward: marriage to the princess of his dream life, who turns out to have been systematically dreaming the same series of dreams as George all these many years.

The dream story reflects the more dangerous underside of his lyrical journey through life and involves a series of journeys into and over progressively threatening landscapes. The basic configuration of the dreamscape includes entrance through a safe outer region guarded by a pile of brushwood and by a street lamp crowning a ridge of high ground, a middle region of valleys and a Sea of Dreams, and a still more dangerous interior with mysterious strangers eating amid roses and gardens in a railway station, and, finally, the mysterious end of the journey—a huge house containing, in its deepest recesses, a Sick Thing.

The entrance to the delightful secret world where "anything was possible" is guarded by two recurring signs—a pile of brushwood and a lamppost, clearly differentiated emblems of femininity and masculinity that mark the boundaries of a day world of recognizable sexual differentiation.

> He would find himself sliding into dreamland by the same road—
> a road that ran along a beach near a pile of brushwood. To the
> right lay the sea, sometimes at full tide, sometimes withdrawn
> to the very horizon; but he knew it for the same sea. By that road
> he would travel over a swell of rising ground covered with short,
> withered grass, into valleys of wonder and unreason.Beyond the
> ridge, which was crowned with some sort of street-lamp, anything
> was possible; but up to the lamp it seemed to him that he knew
> the road as well as he knew the parade-ground.

Beyond these signposts lie worlds of "incommunicable delight . . . glorious, for he felt he was exploring great matters." His unpredictable night world confronts him with a road "eaten away in places" that spans ravines, runs along the edge of precipices, and tunnels its way through endless mountains. The sea, sometimes a lyrical sea of dreams, is often a black and angry sea that rages under a full moon and lashes at him "black, foamless tongues of smooth and glossy rollers." Although he loses himself on unknown seas and slips and slides across many-colored islands, rescue always appears in the form of his brushwood girl, a figure who first comes to life out of an illustrated edition of *Grimm's Fairy Tales*, then takes on the form of a real girl he meets in an Oxford pantomime theater. In the dreams the girl evolves from a childhood fairy tale princess, into his boyhood's AnnieanLouise, then into his young brushwood companion.

Inland lie dark purple downs and mysterious and ever more dangerous territories: "Sometimes he was trapped in mines of vast depth hollowed out of the heart of the world, where men in torment chanted echoing songs; and he heard this person (the brushwood girl) coming along through the galleries, and everything was made safe and delightful." More threatening than either the sea or the mines is the danger from a series of mysterious people referred to as "Them," "They," and "It." First perceived as a "mob of stony white people, all unfriendly" who sit at breakfast tables covered with roses, "They" attempt to separate George from his girl. "It" is a female, a dying Sick Thing that lies in bed in a room reached "through leagues of whitewashed passages," in a huge house "surrounded with gardens all moist and dripping." One endless hot tropic night, the boy and girl find themselves creeping into this huge forbidden house and discovering "It" lying in bed. Georgie knows that the least noise "would unchain some waiting horror" and, in his moment of greatest need for help, is disgusted that his companion is merely a child: " 'What disgraceful folly!' he thought. 'Now she could do nothing whatever if Its head came off.' " When the Thing coughs, the ceiling begins to shatter, "They" come rushing in from all quarters, and George barely manages to drag the girl through the stifling rose gardens, across the Thirty-Mile Ride, to the safety of the down, the lamppost, and the brushwood pile. By the end of the story, as George heads back for England, he dreams his familiar dreams once again. Only this time the dreams are entirely safe: the dream companion is no longer a little girl but a woman with dark hair; "They" for some dreamland reason are now friendly or unthreatening, and their Thirty-Mile Ride is accompanied by underground singing and "no panic" as they repeat their old journey from the brushwood pile through the rose-filled waiting rooms and gardens, past the house of the now dormant Sick Thing.

The waking world, then, is one in which Kipling's protagonist realizes all his fantasies and desires and acquires that ultimate object of desire— Miriam (" 'Sounds Jewish—Miriam.' " " 'Jew! You'll be calling yourself a Jew next. She's one of the Herefordshire Lacys. When her aunt dies—.' " Miriam is class, money, and legitimate aristocracy. Miriam, with her ailing mother, is fatherless, and, by marrying her, George will inherit not only her wealth, but the parental role that would be forbidden to him were her parents active participants in society. Marriage will therefore resolve social and familial contradictions: the son will become the father, and the working soldier will become the aristocrat. This simple and mythic outer story with its light and whimsical tone is meant to compensate for the disturbingly incomplete inner metaphoric journey into the house of the Sick Thing. The inner story also subverts the expectations raised by its form. Twin journeys embedded with a dream story might lead the reader to expect, in the protagonist, changes in perception, self-awareness, or wisdom. But our George learns primarily how to defend himself against external threat without gaining any significant insight into the nature of his hidden fears.

As in the stories of Kipling's own life ("Baa, Baa, Black Sheep" and his autobiography), this story also begins with images of society's natural victim—the child. Part of the intention of this study is to see how that victimization is resolved in another curiously absent theater—India. On the level of dream, we watch the child explore increasingly threatening geographical areas that he attempts at first to control by naming, miniaturizing (Hong Kong and Java become tiny lilies, stepping stones in his path), defining, and displacing, but that grow increasingly uncontrollable. On the waking level, however, we see the boy's encounters with a series of microsocieties in which the disempowered and marginalized child-protagonist gradually assumes a position of centrality and power.

The story begins, "A child of three sat up in his crib and screamed at the top of his voice, his fists clenched and his eyes full of terror." His helplessness is exacerbated by the geographic isolation of his nursery—in the west wing where no one could hear him: "The nurse was talking to a gardener among the laurels." When the housekeeper, whose special pet he is, tries to soothe him by asking what it was that frightened him, the boy answers that a policeman came into the house. The dream by itself does not appear fearful: it is a dream of intrusion by public authority into a private, intimate space; it has its real-life source in an actual meeting with policeman Tisdall on Dowhead that morning. But the original manuscript and typescript of the story suggest that the author edited that which might have been most fearsome to the child. In that unrevised version the child says, " 'It was—it was a policeman. He came in froo the window an' ate the rug! I saw him do it!' " To which the nurse replies, " 'Nonsense Master George. Policemen never come through windows. They live in the Garden just like Ponto. Go to sleep' " (Pierpont Morgan Collection). That added detail of intrusion through a forbidden entrance—the window—to eat forbidden contents—the rug—suggests why the child might wake up terrified: the next object for consumption on the policeman's menu might be the child. That first dream of a boundaryless appetite and of intrusion into a forbidden space will later be displaced or, as Edward Said might put it, "Orientalized." India will become the place of excess undermining the rational control of the

Englishman, who will in turn test his manhood, his character, and his rationality by repeatedly intruding into threatening territory that he will decode, tame, and circumscribe within manageable domains. And within his sequential dream story, he and the brushwood girl will intrude into the house of the Sick Thing "It," whose distant bedroom surrounded by gardens must be a late displacement of his own early geographically remote nursery—and on one level (as in Kafka's dream story "The Country Doctor") he is the sick thing who fears anatomical loss. Only now, that distant marginal room is the central nightmare region of the dream. And on this level the bedroom is both the beginning and the end of one of his many journeys.

When we next see the boy as a child of six, we see how he has learned in part to conquer his three-year-old fear of the night world. He has turned his ability to dream into a "new power . . . a secret," by transposing an unfinished bedtime story told by his mother into a dream in which he becomes the prince, the pasha, and the giant-killer. Rather than fear intrusion, as he did in his first dream, he becomes the intruder entering the forbidden dreamscape through a safe outer region guarded by a pile of brushwood stacked somewhere near a beach. It is a territory casually divided between land and sea, so casually that "ships ran high up the dry land and opened into cardboard boxes; or gilt and green iron railings that surrounded beautiful gardens turned all soft and could be walked through and overthrown so long as he remembered it was only a dream." And because he is in control, he can choose not to be alone is his dreamscape as he had been in his nursery. He peoples it with playing children, and in particular with a brushwood girl whom he names AnnieanLouise, whose magic words " 'Ha! Ha!' said the duck, laughing" rescue the boy from drowning by raising the bottom of the deep as he wades out with a twelve-inch flowerpot on each foot. The boy has acquired the early power to domesticate and control even the depths of the sea.

Our next glimpse of George, at age seven, has him for the first time outside his bed and outside the privacy of his home in an alien world of "the grown-ups whom Georgie tolerated but did not pretend to understand"; this world consists of an enormously fat man who asks if he will eat bread and cheese, a play in which people's heads come flying off, a Provost of Oriel who sleeps in the presence of others, and a lovely little girl in black who looks like Alice in Wonderland. Of these new inhabitants, Georgie likes the last best and shows her his wound, a cut on his thumb, the result of his "most valuable possession"—a savage, triangular knife. This wound, displayed here as a sign of his triumph, is displaced in his dreams onto the Sick Thing. Other features in the outside world—a place in which George cannot

yet act with power—are also dismissed and internalized into his more significant inner life. The grown-ups will become part of the world of "They"
and "Them," and the dark girl will be colonized into his dream life to replace
the earlier golden AnnieanLouise. In both worlds the boy's identity will be
defined in terms of the success with which he can turn a wound into a
triumph, survive in spite of a world inhabited by "They," "Them," and "It."
That the wound is an object of desire in real life and an object of fear in his
dreams suggests the separation in George's life between the outer world and
his inner self—a separation that will increase with age and with the journey
into India.

The next three phases of his life—ten years at an English public school,
Sandhurst, and India—lead to a restructuring of his private inner emotional
life that must be subordinated to the public and external world of school
and games. Now, Home becomes "a far-away country, full of ponies and
fishing and shooting, and men-visitors who interfered with one's plans; but
school was the real world. . . . And Georgie was glad to be back in authority
when the holidays ended." We are also told that school defines for the boy
certain boundaries between that which is discouraged (dreaming and emo-
tions) and that which is encouraged (precision, accuracy, strength). It is
during this third stage then that we see the boy defining a hierarchy of values
to be measured against that which was most "real"—his school. And it is
here that the outer world encroaches upon, contests, and begins its triumph
against the claims of his inner life—a triumph that materializes when George
returns to England to discover that his dream brushwood girl is the real-life
Miriam whom he is destined to marry, thereby renouncing any need for an
inner dream life. It is at this stage that we see the evolution of the Kipling
ideal—discipline, sexual innocence, self-control, the value of the "school
mask," and the upholding of public official policy. If part of the conscious
meaning of the story is that "England's wars are won on the playing fields
of Eton," then George's school must take credit for his triumphs on the
battlefield of Empire.

In India he is the most loved, most sought after, most quoted barrack
authority. In spite of all the designing ladies, George keeps free from the
intrigues of the Indian outpost and from sex: " 'If Cottar only knew it, half
the women in the station would give their eyes—confound 'em—to have the
young 'un in tow.' " His seniors worry about his turning into a "regular
'Auntie Fuss' of an Adjutant," but fate proves him a man by sending him
to fight a "real" war: "Cottar nearly wept with joy as the campaign went
forward. They were fit—physically fit beyond the other troops; they were
good children in camp, wet or dry, fed or unfed; and they followed their

officers with the quick subtleness and trained obedience of a first-class football fifteen."

What is singularly minimized during his heroic combat is India and Indians. We are told, probably concerning the Second Afghan War of 1881, that "fate sent the change that was needed, in the shape of a little winter campaign on the border, which, after the manner of little campaigns, flashed out into a very ugly war; and Cottar's regiment was chosen among the first." George's distance from the reality of war and India (and from the events of his own life) are reflected not only in the increasingly coy use of the third-person omniscient narrator whose voice seems only accidentally related to a boy encountering death and India, but in the curious language exemplified in the passage above. The angle from which the event is perceived is so distant that the horror of war is miniaturized into a "little" campaign, and its only significance seems to be contained within the context of sports— Cottar's regiment was chosen among the first. Those who are to be warred against, subdued, defeated, killed are neither named nor romanticized. They are simply and significantly absent. And India is an empty space, an absence, that serves as a means for progressing from school to life, from the playing fields of Eton to Home, Marriage, and Empire. The war therefore is an excuse to glorify and fortify the men into manliness: " 'Now,' said a major, 'this'll shake the cobwebs out of us all—especially you, Galahad.' " The experience in India allows George to construct a code of personal behavior and leadership based on public school codes that results in the nonsexual commitment to the brotherhood of Empire, in the infantilization of his men into "good children" and a "football fifteen," of a war into a "little" campaign, and of India into an absence. (Native Indians are mentioned once in passing, marginalized into a childlike audience. When Cottar trains his men by racing them across country after a trail of torn paper, "the native population, who had a lust for sport in every form, wished to know whether the white men understood wrestling.") Maturity and character are gained by a colonization of the self—by denial, repression, and mechanization. But once this stage is accomplished, a limited intimacy is allowed:

> "There's no place like England—when you've done your work."
> "That's the proper way to look at it, my son."

But as other Kipling stories have demonstrated, outward success is no guarantee for survival in India; midway through Cottar's phenomenal successes with subordinates, superiors, and women in the army, a major prophesies: "but, then, that's the kind that generally goes the worst mucker in the end." The fear of going "the worst mucker," of disintegrating irrationally and publicly, of being invaded, engulfed, or petrified by threatening others results in the elaborate development of denial and repression in the real world, and a night world haunted with a sexually charged dreamscape whose action mirrors his deepest anxieties.

Those anxieties are provoked by areas of his waking life over which he has no control: home, England, and sex. If school, Sandhurst, and India do not consciously threaten George (as they did Kipling), it is partly because they obey the rules of his defense system and partly because he has displaced onto the language of his dreams that which is most fearsome about them. As opposed to the "real" world of games and war, home is soft, unreal, dreamlike, and relatively scary. If the only way to reconcile these two opposing worlds is through marriage to Miriam, then the main threat to that ultimate reward of union is illicit maternal love. All through his years in India, he is, unknown to himself, threatened with motherly sex—from Mrs. Elery, who complains to a Commander that he is "workin' my nice new boy too hard," to Mrs. Morrison, who admits "*I* want to kiss him. Some day I think I will. Heigh-ho! she'll be a lucky woman that gets Young Innocence," to the designing Mrs. Zuleika, to his actual mother back home. His most threatening sexual encounter takes place on that most instable and uncertain place, a ship at sea, where Mrs. Zuleika with her "motherly" interest speaks of "Love in the abstract" and demands sexual confidences. When George arrives home, it is into the waiting arms of yet another woman—his eager mother, who comes into his bedroom to tuck him up for the night and to ask him leading questions about his nonexistent sex life. After she discovers the incredible (his virginity), "she blessed him and kissed him on the mouth, which is not always a mother's property, and said something to her husband later at which he laughed profane and incredulous laughs."

The sexual anxiety at the heart of this story repeats itself in the recurring flight of the boy from exposure, vulnerability, and danger to a sheltered place of total security, away from the threats of forbidden, motherly relationships toward a safe, mature sexuality. The defense system he establishes against his dangerous fantasy is careful self-control under the magical protection of an internalized fantasy girl, who in his dreams keeps changing ages to remain as remote from the mother as possible. The entire journey carries an implicit Kipling theme: that we mature by escaping maternal love and being "manly" until we find a suitable love object free of material associations, after our colonial characters are built and tested. And someone back home is always watching, censoring, controlling our most dangerous actions, and we must trust that silent watcher in the night as we must our Empire: so later, Miriam admits to dreaming of "another woman—out there on the sea. I saw her." The ordinary adventure story holds its tension and the reader's interest because of the potential threat in store for the protagonist as he encounters his next major test in the real world. Here, however, the boy's triumphs in encountering worldly tests are tediously predictable. The question that remains problematic is if he can cope with and survive the threats of his unconscious life.

This private obsession with the unconscious as a source of terror and fascination lies at the heart of the Kipling myth and informs all his tales. Consequently, almost all his stories involve night journeys into alien realms. But what makes these journeys so idiosyncratic, so typical of Kipling (rather than Conrad or Lawrence), is their timid and guarded nature, their sense of forced continuity and cohesion that constantly represses and conceals elements of disturbance in the text. The outer journey of the wooden, predictable protagonist from England to India and back at first jars against the inner unpredictable dream life—but only for a while. The deus ex machina at the end gives the reader a sense of an ending in narrative and in history that is radiant with confidence. Always in Kipling, tranquility and order will be restored if necessary through a hysterical insistence on forced closure. In this story the closure is charming, the brushwood boy will be saved, rescued from the dangers of his own unconscious, even from his own self—and he will be rescued by a member of the ruling class: a princess. What the story leaves incomplete is the inner journey that simply stops without allowing the boy a final confrontation with the beast in the jungles of his unconscious—the Sick Thing.

Except for the brushwood pile, all other dream elements surrounding the House have their origins in details the boy recalls of waking life. The gardens dripping with roses recall his parents' home, which he finds distant, romantic, vaguely confusing, and threatening. What George finds most threatening at home before his journey to India is his lack of control and the presence of authorities other than his own ("and Georgie was glad to be back in authority when the holidays ended"). After he has earned the rewards of the good colonialist and acquired an armor with which to journey into danger, he returns home to a new acceptance by the previously forbidding adults. His father invites him out on the terrace "to smoke among the roses," and George thinks: " 'Perfect! By Jove, it's perfect!' Georgie was looking at the round-bosomed woods beyond the home paddock, where the white pheasant boxes were ranged; and the golden air was full of a hundred sacred scents and sounds." This sensual, maternal, paradisal landscape is a clear contrast to the threatening feminine landscape of his Indian dreams filled with ravines, precipices, tunnels, black and changeable seas, and gardens overly ripe with moisture, perfume, and song. The Sick Thing—fed by multiply determined, indirect, and contradictory elements—is, however, the most complex symbol in the dream. On a regressive level, the sources in real life are partly George's own mother, partly the sickly, sleepy behavior the seven-year-old George attributed to adults, and partly Miriam's invalid mother—a contribution of her mind. That the unreachable end of this otherwise delicious journey should contain a sick female figure lying in bed with an unstable head ready to fall off at the least provocation suggests that the initial incest anxiety is accompanied by a projected fear of punishment—castration or headlessness. With her vague and oppressive sickness associated with excess heat, and loss of control, the Sick Thing's infantile connections with forbidden and destructive sexuality are later Orientalized and displaced onto that ultimate center of disintegration—India. As child, as fantasy princess, and later as mature woman from a legitimate class, the brushwood girl grows old along with George, thereby representing safe, normal companionship and acceptable sexuality, in contrast to the life-threatening and repellent sexuality of the Sick Thing. So also Army, Sandhurst, and School are the institutionalized counterpart to the princess: they will protect him against the House, the journey through the abyss, or what Kipling elsewhere called "The City of Dreadful Night."

The dream journey also reflects Kipling's characteristic ways of dealing with what R. D. Laing has called the "three forms of anxiety encountered by the ontologically insecure person: engulfment, implosion, petrification." He deals with the fear of engulfment (whose signs are the enclosed, stifling garden and house) by taking along a talisman, a guide, and a legitimate sexual companion; he deals with implosion, or the terrifying sense that at any moment the world might "crash in and obliterate all identity," through control and retreat, by always reminding himself in mid-dream "that he would be safe if he could reach the down with the lamp on it"; and he deals with the fear of petrification, of being turned into stone or dying, by projecting that anxiety onto others, by turning the threatening mother into a thing, by turning his elders into nameless, depersonalized "They" and "Them." Within the larger polarization between his waking world guarded by Policeman Day and his nightworld of dreams exist many other oppositions, the most significant between "They" and "Us." This defining of boundaries and defenses against intrusion by others serves to insulate the Kipling protagonist against "unknown continents" within and without. "Them," "They," "It," and "the mob of stony white people" are all dream objects of petrification caused by the dreamer's need to dehumanize, simplify, and classify Others into stony anonymity in order to control them. George's dream journey might involve perilous crossings over ferocious seas, stony ravines, and sandy deserts, but even then he is sure that there was less danger from the real elements than "from 'Them' whoever 'They' were." The division between Us and Them is also a wish-fulfilling inner division between desire and fear, between the realm of possibilities allowed the boy and the girl when they are a self-contained secret unit, and the restricted realm allowed by the larger world that contains Others.

This division haunts the story on levels of form, imagery, actions, and ideology. The schizophrenic fragmentation of this text into the nonsexual world of action, war, colonial discipline, and empire and the sexual world of dream, desire, freedom, and fear is repeated in both the form and the ideological content of the story. Quite simply, the work of empire is daytime work and therefore incompatible with objects of nighttime desire. Once that fundamental division is accepted and assumed on a private level, then its social implications can be expected to follow. The story of George Cottar, like that of other Kipling protagonists, is that of a young man who has gone through an exemplary Kiplingesque regime of repression, control, and denial in India and can now return to England and its release from discipline, armed against its dangers with "character." In the real world it will allow him to enter threatening colonized spaces like India to test his resistance against immersion in the destructive elements of desire or empathy for the alien Other. His reward for such personal and ideological schizophrenia will be social reconciliation (return to the parental English home, smoking in the garden with father, parties) and union with a significant Other (marriage with the heiress who has appropriately aristocratic English lineage).

II

Although this story is in some ways an anomaly because it is Kipling's only dream story, certain characteristics central to his narrative myth, made explicit here, recur not only in his other fiction but in his autobiography, *Something of Myself*. Written forty-three years after "The Brushwood Boy," this late memoir is perhaps the best illustration of Kipling's recurring patterns of fantasy and defense. It is also a rich source for understanding his earlier fiction because the connections between life and psychological organization are made explicit here and because its patterns of perception, structure, imagery, and ideas are analogous to those in his fiction. For all its factual content, Kipling's autobiography is an account of fundamental fears and of the development of psychological defenses against them. Like some other memoirs by novelists, this work embodies certain personal myths that underlie all his fiction. Those myths involve the need to descend into a physical, psychological, or sexual underworld and there to confront certain idiosyncratic threats. Primarily the Kipling persona fears abandonment and self-loss in the face of chaos, darkness, alcohol, or blindness; he fears passion and madness; he fears the uncanny, the mysterious, or the ghostlike, whose presence signals the "return of the repressed," thereby threatening the sanity of its victims. Against these threats Kipling built a system of defenses out of a code of order, light, conservatism, and art; out of a persona that was at once distant, cool, ironic, and superior; and out of a compulsion to "belong" to an ever growing number of organizations, clubs, and countries. A number of characteristic images that recur in his fiction emerge from this myth; the most persistent is that of a fundamentally divided world—a double life split between day and night, England and India, the conscious and the unconscious, sanity and madness, the civilized and the savage, reality and dream, ship and sea.

His earliest memories of India are divided between the exotic world of his servants, where he spoke and dreamed in Hindi, and the disciplined world of his equally loving parents, where he was expected to speak in English, of days filled with song, stories, and trips to his father's art school and of nights filled with songs and stories told by his Hindu servants. When this Edenic existence is inexplicably and rudely interrupted by a journey over the sea followed by abandonment in England in the "House of Desolation," he finds himself introduced to "Hell . . . in all its terrors," to physical beatings, blindness, and eventually a nervous breakdown. But it is here that he learns certain defenses against disintegration: "it made me give attention to the lies I soon found it necessary to tell: and this, I presume, is the foundation of literary effort." He learns caution, wariness, distrust, and deep admiration for detachment, the art of seeing "from the outside"—defenses that recall not only Kipling's affection for the frame story and the safely distanced older narrator but also Kipling's fear of being trapped inside, engulfed and vulnerable to hostile, threatening reality. His closest friend at school, for instance, is most admired for possessing

> an invincible detachment—far beyond mere insolence—towards all the world: and a tongue, when he used it, dipped in some Irish-blue acid. . . . I think it was his infernal impersonality that swayed us in all our wars and peace. He saw not only us but himself from the outside, and in later life, as we met in India and elsewhere, the gift persisted.

When he returned to India after an absence of ten years, he found his life again divided between his English home, club, and office in working hours and a nocturnal life of wanderings from midnight until dawn through the native underworld of gullies and bazaars when "the night got into my head." In the bazaars he accumulated his esoteric understanding of Indian customs and found his inspiration for his lost Indian epic *Mother Maturin;* it was in his own words "my own place, where I find heat and smells and oils and spices, and puffs of temple incense, and sweat and darkness, and dirt and lust and cruelty, and above all, things wonderful and fascinating innumerable." But his nocturnal willingness to love and to encounter the chaos of India is contradicted by his daytime fears of falling victim to its dangers.

Those dangers are the constant presence of disease and death. He sees young boys living in isolation and dying of either cholera, blood poisoning, or typhoid "mostly at the regulation age of twenty-two"; he lives amid "temper frayed by heat to breaking-point but for sanity's sake held back from the break." He is shot at, offered bribes, and humiliated even by his own government when he realizes the deviousness of British control of the news fit to print in his newspaper. Oppressed by each hot season until he finds himself close to a nervous breakdown ("the edge of all endurance"), Kipling manages at each crisis to save himself. Sometimes that salvation is achieved through hard work (ten to fifteen hours a day even with a temperature of 104); sometimes through the orderly setting around which his daily life revolves—the all male Punjab Club; sometimes through the good-humored, joyful tone of his parents' home filled with love "to sweeten all things"; sometimes through the magic medium of a single book—Walter Besant's *All in a Garden Fair*, about which he writes: "But I *do* know that that book was my salvation in sore personal need, and with the reading and re-reading it became to me a revelation, a hope and strength."

III

Kipling's other fiction and his most persistent narrative stance suggest that his stories are further fictionalized treatments of his central myth. The divided need both to encounter and to retreat from a perilous world resulted in two types of Kipling heroes: the safe, detached narrators who typically tell of fools venturing where frame narrators fear to tread ("The Man Who Would Be King," " 'The Finest Story in the World,' " "Thrown Away," "The Recrudescence of Imray") and helpless protagonists in whose abandonment one can repeatedly detect the reworkings of infantile anxieties ("Baa Baa, Black Sheep," "To Be Filed for Reference," "Consequences," "The Arrest of Lieutenant Golightly," "The Strange Ride of Morrowbie Jukes").

In each of these stories the patterns of dangerous fantasy and defense repeat those of "The Brushwood Boy" and of the autobiography: in order to survive India, the Kipling hero must be constantly on guard, learned in Indian ways, a master of Indian disguise, wary, observant, and cautious. The chief threats to his rigidly defensive stance are many. Primarily he fears disintegration and abandonment in the complex, mysterious, or apparently chaotic nature of the land as manifested in the mystery of alien India, the labyrinthine bureaucracy of colonial India, and the intrigues of colonial women. The compulsion to rework this fear in various modes through the distinct voices of detached observer and victimized participant suggests Kipling's dual need both to confront and to deny its significance.

"Thrown Away," for instance, is one of many painful testing stories about a "Boy" who comes out (unlike George Cottar) ill-equipped to handle displacement and challenge in India. He is not even given a name because he represents legions of sheltered, pretty, petted boys who come out only to die in the colonies. Lacking balance, restraint, or humor, the Boy takes all his losses (gambling, friends, identity, women) too seriously. Some carelessly cruel comment made by a woman seems finally to have been "*the* thing that kicked the beam in the Boy's mind," and he retreats into a distant Rest House to commit suicide.

The technique of this early story is relevant because its narrative voice is typical of so many others: it is related by a reporter equipped with a weary and cynical knowledge of India, a detached efficiency, and a ghoulish sense of humor. He is able to condense an individual tragedy into an ironic universal truth: "There was a Boy once who had been brought up under the 'sheltered life' theory; and the theory killed him dead." Because he has not been desensitized from infancy to humiliation and hostility, the boy, we are told, takes too many things too seriously. But the older narrator knows better and offers the reader the preferred perspective on colonial posts:

> Now India is a place beyond all others where one must not take things too seriously—the midday sun always excepted. . . . Flirtation does not matter, because everyone is being transferred and either you or she leave the Station, and never return. Good work does not matter, because a man is judged by his worst output and another man takes all the credit of his best as a rule. Bad work does not matter, because other men do worse and incompetents hang on longer in India than anywhere else. . . . Sickness does not matter, because it's all in the day's work, and if you die, another man takes over your place and your office in the eight hours between death and burial.

How can the man presumed by so many to be the poet of Empire create such a terrible, cynical vision of colonial possibility? He does it through a narrator whose discourse is designed to transcend real issues and social problems through a language that connects and unifies real divisions by indulging in universal truths. The movement from "one must not take things too seriously" to "nothing matters" is a movement from defensive cynicism to defensive nihilism. To blur real social distinctions is to deny them value; and once he has devalued the colonial situation, the narrator can safely retreat into false universalities. When the narrator and the Major discover the mutilated body of the Boy, the Major breaks down, but the narrator, though touched, continues with the business of clearing up the mess. After the two men decide to stage a fake but more comforting death by cholera for the benefit of his family, and after they substitute for his "dreary, and hopeless and touching" letters some of their own more appropriate ones, the narrator collapses into hysterical laughter: "The laughing-fit and chokes got hold of me again, and I had to stop. The Major was nearly as bad." His uncontrollable laughter, corresponding to the Major's earlier uncontrollable weeping, mirrors the boy's fatal loss of control. Each gesture both exposes and parodies the other: whereas the Major can willingly identify with the Boy's feelings, the narrator defends himself against the possibility through grotesque laughter. An increasingly layering and regressive effect may be seen in the relationship between the narrator, the older Major, and the Boy himself. Just as the Boy's suicide reminds the Major of his fears ("He said that he himself had once gone into the same Valley of the Shadow as the Boy, when he was young and new to the country; so he understood how things fought together in the Boy's poor jumbled head"), so the Major's collapse into tears reminds the narrator of his vulnerability. Both the Boy and the Major in varying degrees threaten the workable defenses the narrator has erected against the possibility of regression and self-loss. But because the narrator seems determined to point out the contrast between himself and the suicide, the story of the Boy becomes the outward sign of the unacknowledged fears of the narrator.

Another important maturation and testing story that illustrates the development of defenses against maternal threat and the unconscious is " 'The Finest Story in the World.' " Its narrative structure, a frame story, has two storytellers, an older and a younger writer who serve as doubles for each other. The tale is ostensibly about Charlie Mears, a twenty-year-old banking clerk who suffers from literary aspirations: "He rhymed 'dove' with 'love' and 'moon' with 'June' and devoutly believed that they had never so been rhymed before." One day, however, Charlie charges into the narrator's presence inflamed with a "notion that would make the most splendid story that was ever written." As his story haltingly unfolds, the narrator realizes that what Charlie Mears is recalling are in fact past experiences in previous incarnations: when he was a slave on the lowest deck of a Greek galley, and later when he served on a Viking ship that went to America. When the narrator repeats this tale to a Hindu friend, he is told that such remembrances do occur, though usually "the door is shut," but that they will undoubtedly cease as soon as Charlie meets a girl. True to the prediction, the story ends with Charlie falling in love with a "tobacconist's assistant with a weakness for pretty dress" and scorning the narrator's attempts to remind him of the finest story in the world that now would never be written.

This is Kipling's most "uncanny" story. Just as Freud has explained the uncanny by connecting it with the return of the repressed, with the idea of a double, with "regression to a time when the ego was not yet sharply differentiated from the external world and from other persons," so the structural doubling of storytellers compels the older narrator to relive his early fears and anxieties through the younger. The story of reincarnation here serves the same function that the dream does in "The Brushwood Boy": both are metaphors for the unconscious. What Charlie Mears is uncannily remembering is not merely previous incarnations but his own unconscious life: his life in the womb, his birth and latency. He remembers two lives—one claustrophobic and one open and free. His claustrophobic life chained as a slave to an oar in the dark lower deck of a Greek galley is followed by a battle at sea and death by drowning. He recalls in graphic images the death of a man "cut up in his chains and stuffed through the oarhole in little pieces." Further reminders of the birth trauma occur during the narrator's questioning of Charlie. Asked if he remembers what the water level looked like just before it burst upon him, Charlie replies: "It looked just like a banjo-string drawn tight, and it seemed to stay there for years." After this death he lives once again. But this new life (recalling the liberation of latency) is one of adventure: he tells of sailing an open galley, of sunsets on the open sea, of exploring new woods in new islands, of sailing to America as a red-haired hero on an open ship, and of being cheered on by a red-haired godlike leader. But Charlie's uncanny memories fade as he enters maturity and genital sexuality with his first love: " 'Isn't it—isn't it wonderful?' he whispered, pink to the tips of his ears, wrapped in the rosy mystery of first love. 'I didn't know; I didn't think—it came like a thunderclap.' " And the narrator muses: "Grish Chunder was right. Charlie had tasted the love of woman that kills remembrance, and the finest story in the world would never be written."

The question that remains is why the "Lords of Life and Death," who normally allow "nothing to escape that might trouble or make uneasy the minds of men," leave open the gates to the memory of Charlie Mears. The answer must lie in the boy's as yet unresolved and infantile fixation to his mother. In the first sentence of the story, the boy is introduced as "the only son of his mother who was a widow." When Charlie later plays in the billiard salon, the narrator suggests that he "go back to his mother." We learn that mother does not encourage the son's literary aspirations, that his writing table at home is the edge of his washstand, and that he fears his mother's judgment. In response to a compliment made by the narrator, Charlie inadvertently lets slip a half-phrase that reveals his awareness of a threatening maternal bond: " 'Do you think so?' he answered with a pleased flush. 'I often tell myself that there's more in me than my mo—than people think.' " He evolves into maturity with the discovery of first love, with his loss of contact with the unconscious, and with his subsequent renunciation of mother. To the narrator's not-so-innocent inquiry at his mother's reaction to his girlfriend, the boy confidently replies, "I don't care a damn what she says."

The relationship between the Kipling narrator and Charlie Mears is significant for an understanding of narrative voice in all Kipling's frame tales. In *Something of Myself* Kipling built an identity in India by becoming a literary personality, by using the distancing of art not as escape but as a means to control reality. Language and literature were used as major defenses against maternal threats of engulfment and self-loss. In " 'The Finest Story in the World' " the boy serves as an "uncanny" double for the older man by reminding him of his earlier mental stages, his own anxieties that the narrator has learned to control through the defense of art and style. Consequently, though he willingly draws attention to the wonder of the real Charlie Mears in touch with his deepest self, he must also constantly remind the reader of the boy's gaucheries—his absurd literary yearnings, his inability to write coherently, his tasteless poetry, his general ignorance, and his trashy girlfriend. In other frame stories, such as "The Man Who Would Be King," a similar narrator sits in his office, distant, ironic, and judgmental, while he cheerfully creates doubles—Dravot and Carnehan—to act out his most fearsome fantasies.

Within this context of autobiography and fiction, "The Brushwood Boy" is particularly significant because here, if not in his other tales, Kipling abandons his usual defense of the frame and risks an unusual descent into the dream life of the brushwood boy. Yet through this divided world of dream and reality, night and day, echo Kipling's recurring obsession with private fears disguised by an elaborate public defense.

In his autobiography Kipling refers several times to Browning's Fra Lippo Lippi as a "not too remote ancestor," to "young Lippo, whose child I was," and prefaces his third chapter, "Seven Years Hard," with the words:

> I am poor Brother Lippo by your leave.
> You need not clap your torches to my face.

It is not difficult to see Kipling's kinship with Lippi as analogous to his kinship with his fictional dream self, the brushwood boy. Brother Lippi also led a life divided between his daytime identity as a life-denying monk cloistered within his monastic cell and his nighttime identity as a street urchin and artist of the profane. Doomed to an eternally divided life, Lippi tries in his art to reconcile his conflicts between the earthly and the divine. And so his *Coronation of the Virgin* includes not only portraits of real mistresses of Priors but also, as a daring self-referring finale, a portrait of himself—"I, caught up with my monk's things by mistake"—violating the "pure company" with yet another reminder of the disturbed connections between life and art, flesh and spirit, the profane and the sacred. Kipling saw in Lippi yet another divided nightwalker who, no more than Kipling, could succeed in reconciling, through art, a divided consciousness.

DAVID BROMWICH

Kipling's Jest

Two of Kipling's stories, "Wireless" and "Dayspring Mishandled," have a special bearing on his poetry, for they treat the notion of unconscious genius with a drastic literalness. The heroes of both stories are writers innocent of the contents of their own minds. In "Wireless," a cockney pharmacist falls into a trance and writes out several ecstatic passages from "The Eve of St. Agnes"; or rather he composes them, laboriously, as if for the first time: he has never read the poem and his interests are confined to his trade. Yet he loves a woman like Fanny Brawne, and he is consumptive. We are left with the matter-of-fact suggestion that, all circumstances being favorable, a citizen of modern London became an accidental passenger on a journey he never booked. In "Dayspring Mishandled," a hack journalist writes for his amusement some verses of Chaucerian pastiche. The result proves useful many years later, when, having disguised his invention, he arranges for it to surface as a fragment of an undiscovered *Canterbury Tale*, with the aim of embarrassing a lifelong rival who has assumed a venerable place among Chaucerian scholars. Bits of the tale are quoted: they are captivating in themselves and, after the glosses have been added, irrefutable. The scholar is of course taken in, though the story ends ambiguously, with his folly still unexposed. It may be noticed that two separate processes are at work in these confusions of identity. The young man who seemed to be a second Keats really was one for a moment, whereas the hack could rise above himself only by feigning another writer's effects. But it is not clear that this difference counts for much with Kipling; and in any case the stories

From *Grand Street* 4, no. 2 (Winter 1985). © 1985 by David Bromwich and Grand Street Publications, Inc.

share a curious premise. They ask us to think of inspiration as closely related to forgery.

Kipling himself believed that all his writing was done at the command of a personal Daemon—a conception that shifts the emphasis slightly. We know so little of the Daemon's activity that it may operate under any number of aliases without our guessing the identity that unites them. Style, I think Kipling would have allowed, is the verbal character of an individual, expressed in a marked but variable idiom. But for him the individual is the most doubtful of these elements: when poetry is doing its work rightly, we forget the poet and hear a style talking to an audience. This concern with impersonality, as well as the ideal of direct emotional power, suggests a connection between his way of thinking and T. S. Eliot's; and if one reads more than a few of Kipling's poems with this in mind, one sees that the resemblance is deep and not at all capricious. Kipling had an imaginative as well as a technical interest in certain experiments. It occurred to him, for example, that an ironic contrast might be shaped in verse without an ironic voice, by deploying the same tone for different families of words.

> This is the State above the Law.
>   The State exists for the State alone.
> (This is a gland at the back of the jaw
>   And an answering lump by the collar-bone.)

Those lines were written in 1918, by a poet still learning and still widening his craft, about the time of "Sweeney Among the Nightingales." Yet the affinity covers a range of instances; the most facile line Eliot ever wrote was also a Kipling line, with an imaginable context in the ballads:

> Not with a bang but a whimper,
> Not with a shout but a simper,
> The gentle ladies of Lahore expired over tea.
> *But* the soldiers on the hill—O, the soldiers on the hill.

In the same way Eliot's phrases often wish for a second and demotic life whose name is Kipling.

Whatever mode he elected to work in, Kipling was obviously a great writer of some kind. Many critics have been able to concede this without giving up a general disdain for his achievement (which could be brought in to serve estimates of better authors, as a lowest common factor of genius). Here Eliot's is both a typical and an exceptional case, and it seems to me worth pausing over. In the 1941 introduction to *A Choice of Kipling's Verse*, he called Kipling a unique writer of verse, putting much weight on "unique" and asserting that verse was a thing apart from poetry. The reason one can still feel the need for some such description is that Kipling remains an uneasy experience for the literate. The problem is not his politics. Nor is it the vulgarity of his social judgments: where these are important and have worn badly, we do not read him, but the trouble comes when we do read him with pleasure. He seems willing to succeed in a dozen separate manners and to associate himself with none of them particularly. By his very success, he puts an unaccustomed pressure on the modern ideal of originality, since in his work we glimpse the ideal under a foreign aspect. Kipling cherishes, as do his successors, a language that enters the world already distant and already valuable, even to the point of unannounced parody and quotation. But his long career shows that such qualities may be consistent with the demands of public speech. What he made of this knowledge is an embarrassment for others besides himself, above all for those modernists who took the opposite path, into an almost anonymous private speech.

Eliot came close to saying this in a 1919 review in the *Athenaeum*, where he spoke at length about poetry and its audiences. The article is less positive, but also less condescending, than the later one I have mentioned. It starts by declaring that Kipling's poetry is "in fact, the poetry of oratory; it is music just as the words of orator or preacher are music; they persuade, not by reason, but by emphatic sound." The judgment may be felt to suppress— to acknowledge and depreciate without ever stating—a major fact about Kipling, his familiarity with the moods of the music hall. When, elsewhere in the review, Eliot does allude to this, he seems partly to admire; as the author of "*Under the bam / Under the boo / Under the bamboo tree*" ought naturally to admire; but on the whole he mingles contempt and self-conscious fondness with a dandyish impeccability: "The eighteenth century was in part cynical and in part sentimental, but it never arrived at complete amalgamation of the two feelings. Whoever makes a study of the sentimentalism of the nineteenth century will not neglect the peculiar cynical sentiment of Mr. Kipling. In a poem like Mr. Kipling's 'The Ladies,' the fusion is triumphant." Notice, in the second sentence, the transition from "sentimentalism" to "sentiment." The latter has an honorable history—"sentiments to which every bosom returns an echo." And the audience of the music hall, as Eliot came to believe, were right in caring for just such sentiments as one finds in Kipling's poems. Yet by treating the two words as synonyms, he gives the whole comment a pejorative sound.

Nothing was more important to Kipling's appeal than his mastery of common sentiments. His self-knowledge here leaves very little for a critic to expose; in "My Great and Only," a prose sketch about writing a song that pleased, he reports: "I clung to the Great Heart of the People—my people—four hundred 'when it's full, Sir.' I had not studied them for nothing." Some way in, the song begins to catch; a few verses more and it brings down the house: "Who shall tell" (reflects Kipling) "the springs that move masses? I had builded better than I knew. . . . They do not call for authors on these occasions, but I desired no need of public recognition. I was placidly happy." Eliot would consent to be overheard by such "masses," in return for the privilege of overhearing them, but to write *for* them was at once below his ambition and above it. In the review itself, however, a contrast between his own attitude and Kipling's is only implied, by his pairing of Kipling and Swinburne as poets who deal with ideas as their stock in trade. Against them stands a figure like Conrad—or, we may suppose, Eliot—who has no ideas but "a point of view, a world; it can hardly be defined, but it pervades his work and is unmistakable." This appears to exclude Kipling so firmly that one is puzzled to reconcile it with the review's closing thought:

> And yet, Mr. Kipling is very nearly a great writer. There is an unconsciousness about him which, while it is one of the reasons why he is not an artist, is a kind of salvation. . . . It is wrong, of course, of Mr. Kipling to address a large audience; but it is a better thing than to address a small one. The only [still] better thing is to address the hypothetical Intelligent Man who does not exist and who is the audience of the Artist.

We are left without any satisfying rival to Kipling's kind of greatness. There may be something hypothetically better. But the phrase "who does not exist" and the mocking upper-case letters (very different from Kipling's "Great Heart of the People") cheat us of any hope that the possibility may be realized.

The weakest element in this review is the use it makes of Conrad. For, if one compares similar stories by Conrad and Kipling—"The Lagoon," say, with "At the End of the Passage"—it is plain that Conrad writes with a more impressively on-purpose air, but it does not follow that his is the higher dedication. Thus, where Eliot believed he was separating art from non-art, he seems actually to have been recording a preference as to the proper stance for an artist. He admires the sort of artist who has nobody to convince: the modern, because he is undecided among beliefs; the medieval, because he is bound to a total system of belief. If, in Kipling's defense, one notices that "The Lagoon" and "At the End of the Passage" are stories about empire and that "At the End of the Passage" is the better story, it may still be replied that Conrad would be shocked to see his story read as an expression of empire ideas, whereas Kipling doubtless would not be shocked. But this is only a restatement of the fact in different words; it means that Kipling always has a house to bring down. For him, each new audience occupies a position like that of the listener in "Wireless" or the scholar in "Dayspring Mishandled." The artist, in short, works to convince the audience; the audience, simply by being there, serves to authenticate the artist. To take part in such an exchange may betray a mercenary complacency. But in Kipling this continual testing of his effects seems to be another form of restlessness. He is a virtuoso of nerves, a master tactician of the not-yet-commonplace. His success remains perpetually in question because it upsets the usual distinction between poetry and rhetoric—divisions of the larger category of writing, which, in his period and ours, have carried conviction as moral opposites. Kipling's refusal to accept the distinction, his poetry's refusal to be embarrassed by it, make him an unwelcome second self of the modernist. This I think is what Eliot recognized but did not want to say.

In his autobiography, *Something of Myself*, Kipling offers the following remarks on style:

> I made my own experiments in the weights, colours, perfumes,
> and attributes of words, either as read aloud so that they may
> hold the ear, or, scattered over the page, draw the eye. There is
> no line of my verse or prose which has not been mouthed till the
> tongue made all smooth.

The tone is unexpectedly Paterian. But then, why unexpectedly? With lines like "Dominion over palm and pine" or "On dune and headland sinks the fire," Kipling wrote with the disciples of Pater as much in view as the disciples of Cecil Rhodes. Meditation on "the weights, colours, perfumes, and attributes of words" may be felt in every syllable of "Recessional." As poet and as rhetorician, what Kipling seeks is authority: he takes the measure of words, for the sake of persuasions that will occur as if in his absence. This helps to explain his interest in the ballad tradition, with its careful anonymity and automatic claim to authority; and it seems pertinent that forgery was always at home in that tradition. Kipling's bad poems are ventriloquized copies of a style that never existed.

Looking for other poets to compare him with, one may arrive at a list of ballad writers and regional writers, the popular wing of the romantic movement and some newer energetic second-raters: Scott, Campbell, Tom Moore, Hood, Gilbert and perhaps Henley (for whom Kipling professed the highest admiration). However, searching his poems for their footsteps, one is brought back again and again to a different company: Swinburne, Browning, Emerson and Byron. The style of the young Kipling—his ground note,

apart from occasional poems and poems written in dialect—is fairly close to
this:

> O'er the marsh where the homesteads cower apart the harried
>   sunlight flies,
> Shifts and considers, wanes and recovers, scatters and sickens
>   and dies—
> An evil ember bedded in ash—a spark blown west by the
>   wind . . .
> We are surrendered to night and the sea—the gale and the tide
>   behind.

Without the anomalous word, "homesteads," it could be mistaken for the
Swinburne of the *Poems and Ballads*, right down to the echoes of Shelley.
The debt is confessed more openly elsewhere: "I stayed the sun at noon to
tell / My way across the waste of it; / I read the storm before it fell / And
made the better haste of it." This in turn can sink into burlesque, as when
Kipling adapts a celebrated chorus from *Atalanta in Calydon*, and, to Swinburne's Volatile Metaphors ("Before the beginning of years / There came to
the making of man / Time, with a gift of tears; / Grief, with a glass that
ran"), he replies with Crystallized Facts: "Before the beginning of years /
There came to the rule of the State / Men with a pair of shears, / Men with
an estimate."

Yet it is hard to calculate the distance between parody and a kind of
inadvertent homage which only begins as parody. "To the Unknown Goddess" certainly has for its pretext Swinburne's "Hymn to Proserpine":

> Have I met you and passed you already, unknowing,
>   unthinking, and blind?
> Shall I meet you next season at Simla, O sweetest and best of
>   your kind?
>
> Does the P. & O. bear you meward, or, clad in short frocks in
>   the west,
> Are you growing the charms that shall capture and torture the
>   heart in my breast?
>
> Will you stay in the Plains till September—my passion as
>   warm as the day?
> Will you bring me to book on the Mountains, or where the
>   thermantidotes play?

Even here, what Kipling takes with "meward" he gives back with properties more truly his than Swinburne's: the P. & O., the Plains, "passion as warm as the day." By the end of the poem, all one can say is that somehow it has become Kipling's own. The provocation of the ur-Hymn's last phrase, "death is a sleep," is charitably passed over, yet from the general atmosphere of mimicry Kipling invents a fresh mood of wakeful acceptance.

> Ah Goddess! child, spinster, or widow—as of old on Mars Hill
>   when they raised
> To the God that they knew not an altar—so I, a young pagan,
>   have praised
>
> The Goddess I know not nor worship; yet, if half that men tell
>   me be true,
> You will come in the future, and therefore these verses are
>   written to you.

The last couplet is a free man's pontification that happens to fit the require-ments of the poem, answering Swinburne's regret of the lost goddess with a faith in the still-to-be-found.

A better managed influence, Browning, may be heard in a straight-Kipling poem, "One Viceroy Resigns," with a stunning completeness of effect.

> So here's your Empire. No more wine then? Good.
> We'll clear the Aides and Khitmutgars away.
> (You'll know that fat old fellow with the knife—
> He keeps the Name Book, talks in English, too,
> And almost thinks himself the government.)
> O, Youth, Youth, Youth! Forgive me, you're so young.

One has to look closely at the end-stopped lines (a habit of prose workmanship Kipling held onto in verse), with the consequent lack of variation in the breathing pauses, before one feels sure it is only a case of somebody doing Browning. Yet there is a tone of sincere moral bluster that is native to both poets. It accounts for Kipling's decision to write "The Lesson"—the small change of several full-scale jeremiads on the Boer War—in a style of relaxed monologue that might be supposed to follow after "No more wine then?"

> Let us admit it fairly, as a business people should,
> We have had no end of a lesson: it will do us no end of good.

The gruff but well-contented harangue marks a common ground between Bishop Blougram and the ordinary hanger-on of empire.

Kipling spoke with pride of two circumstances respecting the poems he published during the last years of the century: he gave them directly to the *Times*, where they could help to shape public feeling; and he took pay for none of them. He thought of himself as a propagandist, that is, a propagator of morals. But the partisan whose loyalty to a cause is least in question may be granted a certain license—just as the best athlete of a team is allowed the most cutting sarcasms. Kipling makes very full use of his privilege in battle poems:

> A scrimmage in a Border Station—
> A canter down some dark defile—
> Two thousand pounds of education
> Drops to a ten-rupee jezail—
> The Crammer's boast, the Squadron's pride,
> Shot like a rabbit in a ride!
>
> No proposition Euclid wrote
> No formulae the text-books know
> Will turn the bullet from your coat,
> Or ward the tulwar's downward blow.
> Strike hard who cares—shoot straight who can—
> The odds are on the cheaper man.

The abrupt phrases are so consistent that the title, "Arithmetic on the Frontier," can add only a rather pedantic irony. In pace as well as detail, the Byronic *flânerie* of battle is done to perfection here; and Kipling's success, like Byron's, owes much to the play of exotic names ("jezail," "tulwar") and toneless terms ("proposition," "formulae") against the assurance of the public-school vernacular ("shot," "blow," "odds," "cheaper").

The freedom of such writing from sonorous insincerities may itself be displayed with a cheapening pride. In the same attitude under slightly different circumstances, Lionel Johnson, an early and sympathetic reviewer, was offended by the swagger of the unshockable man:

> Angry with foolish shamefacedness, [Mr. Kipling] adopts a foolish shamelessness. Rather than let his work win its way by the subtle power of its ideas, he prefers to force our attention by the studied abruptness of his phrases. It is characteristic of the times: General Booth and Mr. Stanley, the German Emperor and General Boulanger, have done the same thing in practical affairs. But Mr. Kipling, in his profession, is a greater man than they in theirs.

It is true that Kipling avoids ever presenting a situation in which a sense of shame might lead to wisdom; and what he calls wisdom is often merely a return to an instinctive antipathy. But for all that, his sympathies do not seem to me at all predictable. He saw General Booth once at Invercargill near Australia, having first caught a glimpse of him "walking backward in the dusk over the uneven wharf, his cloak blown upwards, tulip-fashion, over his grey head, while he beat a tambourine in the face of the singing, weeping, praying crowd who had come to see him off." When they met later on the P. & O., Kipling complained of the scene on the wharf, but found that Booth refused to share his feelings of delicacy: "Young feller, if I thought I could win *one* more soul to the Lord by walking on my head and playing the tambourine with my toes, I'd—I'd learn how." In recounting the incident Kipling says only that Booth "had the right of it"; but plainly he is glad to show the evidence that Booth was a great man. I believe the sensation of discoveries like these is inseparable from the appeal of Kipling's imperialism.

A man, in his profession, interests Kipling not for his ability to conquer other men, but for his wit in subduing things to a human scheme. The saying often at the back of Kipling's mind is Emerson's "Things are in the saddle / And ride mankind"—a phrase from the "Ode Inscribed to W. H. Channing," which evokes the condition Kipling is always fighting against. Indeed, the Channing ode appears to be the source of one of the strangest and most powerful of all his imperialist poems, the elegy for Joseph Chamberlain called "Things and the Man." Literally this poem is about South Africa and Chamberlain. Morally it is a lesson in the pursuit of empire by which spiritual laws may some day become facts.

> The peace of shocked foundations flew
>   Before his ribald questionings.
> He broke the Oracles in two,
>   And bared the paltry wires and strings.
> He headed desert wanderings;
>   He led his soul, his cause, his clan
> A little from the ruck of Things.
>   *"Once on a time there was a Man."*

Now, who, on hearing the sixth and seventh lines out of context would ever suppose that they were written by Kipling? They suggest an idea that seems in principle beyond his reach—that the mere noise of fame is a low thing; that the hero is someone who leads his people not to the top of a heap, but—"A little from the ruck of Things." The words have an Arnoldian sound, and I have looked for words like them in "The World and the Quietest" and other poems by Arnold, without success. Arnold, of course, writes of practical power deferentially while renouncing any claim to its gifts. But the difference between these poets has in fact very little to do with sensibility, and much to do with the kind of energies they are ready to encourage, whether in imagination or in practice. Kipling values something larger than the world but believes it can be known only by the world's equals. His attitude is usually conceived to be the less poetic one. The truth is that it is the less common one among those whom the world turns out as poets.

Johnson again, in a review of *Barrack-Room Ballads*, picked out a false note of bravado in Kipling's emphasis on deeds.

> This glorification of the Strong, the Virile, the Robust, the Vigorous, is fast becoming as great a nuisance and an affectation as were the True and the Beautiful years ago. It is so easy to bluster and brag; so hard to remember that "they also serve who only stand and wait." Indeed, there seems to be no virtue which Mr. Kipling would not put under the head of valour; virtue, to him, is *virtus*, and all the good qualities of man are valorous. From that point of view, saints and sinners, soldiers and poets, men of science and men of art, if they excel in their chosen works, are all strong men.

But one may as well turn this around; for Kipling has meant to be as tolerant as the "point of view" he implies; only the word *strength* is misleading. If he praises men of different kinds for being similarly strong, he means that they are diversely noble in their work. Yet he needs a way of saying that noble works make secret kin of all who perform them: strength is a fair, but inadequate, choice, just as other choices would be.

In this Kipling writes as a follower of Ruskin. Any craft or project, seriously pursued as a calling, has for him the quality of a moral good: he takes pleasure in the faith of the attempt even more than the use of the result, and writes to communicate his pleasure. It is characteristic that he should have produced, for "The Song of the Banjo," verses close in spirit to the elegy for Chamberlain. Thus in a setting of sheer frolic, with many *Tinka-tinka-tinka-tinka-tinks* and *Plunka-lunka-lunka-lunka-lunks*, one comes at last to the challenge:

> Let the organ moan her sorrow to the roof—
> I have told the naked stars the Grief of Man!
> Let the trumpet snare the foeman to the proof—
> I have known Defeat, and mocked it as we ran!
> My bray ye may not alter nor mistake
> When I stand to jeer the fatted Soul of Things.

Such echoes of the great in the small are an offense against good taste (if good taste be allowed to decide on the great). They confirm a suspicion that still clings to the magic of Kipling's rhetoric, which has lifted poems of both sorts equally, with an undistinguishing touch. This thoughtless generosity he defended only once—"There are nine and sixty ways of constructing tribal lays, / And every single one of them is right!" But on reflection the words turn out to be more a rebuke than an apology.

It is in passing from the tribe to the civilization that Kipling may appear to fail unanswerably. "In his earliest time," Henry James observed in a letter, "I thought he perhaps contained the seeds of an English Balzac. But I have given that up in proportion as he has come down steadily from the simple in subject to the more simple—from the Anglo-Indians to the natives, from the natives to the Tommies, from the Tommies to the quadrupeds, from the quadrupeds to the fish, and from the fish to the engines and screws." Kipling's movement, however, was not solely in this direction, and not more so in his later than is his earlier years. Besides, a single motive guided him throughout. The transition, as he conceived it, between the tribe and the civilization, was a small and always imperceptible affair, hardly more than a formalism on the refined. On this subject particularly Kipling requires a patience that his whole manner seems to resist. The following poem will be found in the Definitive Edition under the simple title "Ode," with the attached explanation "1934: Melbourne Shrine of Remembrance." It appears to have been commissioned for a monument to the war dead of Australia.

> So long as memory, valour, and faith endure,
>   Let these stones witness, through the years to come
> How once there was a people fenced secure
>   Behind great waters girdling a far home.
>
> Their own and their land's youth ran side by side
>   Heedless and headlong as their unyoked seas—
> Lavish o'er all, and set in stubborn pride
>   Of judgment, nurtured by accepted peace.
>
> Then, suddenly, war took them—seas and skies
>   Joined with the earth for slaughter. In a breath
> They, scoffing at all talk of sacrifice,
>   Gave themselves without idle words to death.
>
> Thronging as cities throng to watch a game
>   Or their own herds move southward with the year,
> Secretly, swiftly, from their ports they came,

So that before half earth had heard their name
　　Half earth had learned to speak of it with fear;

Because of certain men who strove to reach,
　　Through the red surf, the crest no man might hold,
And gave their name for ever to a beach
　　Which shall outlive Troy's tale when Time is old;

Because of horsemen, gathered apart and hid—
　　Merciless riders whom Megiddo sent forth
When the outflanking hour struck, and bid
　　Them close and bar the drove-roads to the north;

And those who, when men feared the last March flood
　　Of Western war had risen beyond recall,
Stormed through the night from Amiens and made good,
　　At their glad cost, the breach that perilled all.

Then they returned to their desired land—
The kindly cities and plains where they were bred—
Having revealed their nation in earth's sight
So long as sacrifice and honour stand,
And their own sun at the hushed hour shall light
　　The shrine of these their dead.

Notwithstanding some commonplace touches I find this greatly moving. Like "Recessional," it is public without presumption. It reveals a marked change from the language of that poem; and the change is not entirely for the better: "made good, / At their glad cost, the breach that perilled all" is antique writing, as it means to be, but close to Macaulay's imitation of the antique. Yet the phrase "nurtured by accepted peace" is both fine and modern in its understatement, and there are many such phrases in the poem.

　　Recall that the year is 1934. We can easily forget what it means for an inquisitive mind to remain in the world so long. Kipling, I believe, when he wrote this ode, had been reading the later Yeats—"Because of certain men," "Because of horsemen, gathered apart and hid," "Half earth had learned to speak of it with fear," "Which shall outlive Troy's tale when Time is old." And curiously, the style of "Coole Park and Ballylee" and "Nineteen Hundred and Nineteen" proves at home in the texture of these lines. This is the sort of thing about which the history of poetry can say only that it ought not to happen. It can be explained, however, by an appeal to the history of rhetoric. Kipling and Yeats in their different ways were both of the school of Burke. More particularly, they were distrustful of political reasoners, and sympathized with a social order whose claims they had imagined from within. Defenses of an establishment tend to be a matter of reflex. But neither Kipling's nor Yeats's was: their attachments, being in some measure late found, were deliberate rather than merely habitual. As Yeats's career was haunted by his discovery of loyal patronage among an aristocracy who were supposed not to exist any longer, so Kipling's was haunted by memories of the Indian Mutiny which, eight years before his birth, had given a terrible actuality to the Law. His story "The Head of the District" makes it clear that he interpreted the episode in the light of a simple moral: such things happen when authority is relaxed. What he witnessed of the Boer War seemed to confirm his fears; he called it "a first-class dress parade for Armageddon."

Since Burke's time the grand style, in poetry as in prose, has been the weapon of an established order that sees itself passing from strength to weakness. In a poem like Kipling's "Ode" the larger elegiac story is presumed. The encouragement that he does take from his subject may be owing to the circumstances of the Australian sacrifice. The more obvious of these he notices in saying that the "certain men" came of a protected people, by their remoteness made safe from all but an abstract threat. But the ode gains its effect as well from the force of something unsaid. That the citizens of "the kindly cities and plains," not kindly themselves but speculators, main-chance men, the exiled of the empire, should have joined cause with *his* dead: this makes the occasion personal to Kipling. A reward of associating these political and familiar sentiments may be traced in the Latinate elegance of the fourth stanza, where the syntactical inversion and inward repetitions announce the very distress that the similes are working to conceal, or hoping anyway to subdue to the order of natural fact: "Thronging as cities throng to watch a game / Or their own herds move southward with the year / Secretly, swiftly, from their ports they came." The most striking feature of the poem is the scheme of *anacoluthon* with which it ends, or rather fails to find an end except in feeling. The grammar of the last stanza flows into two channels, in one of which "So long as" appears to govern everything after, while in the other "honour stand" completes the sense and the rest is a murmured blessing.

I want now to compare Kipling's eloquence with Burke's; and the most convincing specimen for this purpose is the summing up, in the "Letter to a Noble Lord," of Burke's attack on the French system of things. From a long survey of the enemy, we are brought back to England and her fortifications:

Such are *their* ideas, such *their* religion, and such *their* law. But as to *our* country and *our* race, as long as the well-compacted

structure of our Church and State, the sanctuary, the holy of
holies of that ancient law, defended by reverence, defended by
power, a fortress at once and a temple, shall stand inviolate on
the brow of the British Sion,—as long as the British monarchy,
not more limited than fenced by the orders of the state, shall,
like the proud Keep of Windsor, rising in the majesty of proportion, and girt with the double belt of its kindred and coeval
towers, as long as this awful structure shall oversee and guard
the subjected land,—so long the mounds and dikes of the low,
fat, Bedford level will have nothing to fear from all the pick-axes
of all the levellers of France. As long as our sovereign lord the
king, and his faithful subjects, the lords and commons of this
realm,—the triple cord which no man can break,— to solemn,
sworn, constitutional frank-pledge of this nation,—the firm guar-
anties of each other's being and each other's rights,—the joint
and several securities, each in its place and order, for every kind
and every quality of property and of dignity,—as long as these
endure, so long the Duke of Bedford is safe, and we are all safe
together,—the high from the blights of envy and the spoliations
of rapacity, the low from the iron hand of oppression and the
insolent spurn of contempt. Amen! and so be it! and so it will
be,—

Dum domus Aeneae Capitoli immobile saxum
Accolet, imperiumque pater Romanus habebit.

Every trick of amplification is employed, and every one serves to advance
the argument, so that we feel the passage itself "rise in the majesty of
proportion." The main device of balance is a series of pairs: "Church and
State," "not more limited than fenced," "oversee and guard," "each other's
being and each other's rights," "joint and several securities," "place and
order," "the high from the blights of envy" and "the low from the insolent
spurn of contempt." And yet this progression is so instinctive, so much a
matter of following cues which the writing can hear itself lay down, that
"the low, fat, Bedford level" is immediately picked up by the ironic echo of
"all the levellers in France." So, again, the three adjectives together prompt
"the triple cord which no man can break," and then with our attention fixed
a clear Amen: "the solemn, sworn, constitutional frank-pledge of this nation."
Kipling, it may be admitted, is too confident with the light arms of the
skirmisher ever to attempt a sentence like that.

Nevertheless, his poetry can sustain effects of gentleness and power at once which make the comparison far from absurd. Consider a well-known passage from "The Islanders," written after the withdrawal of English sentiment from the Boer War, and addressed to a people complacently assured of all that guards them.

Ancient, effortless, ordered, cycle on cycle set,
Life so long untroubled, that ye who inherit forget
It was not made with the mountains, it is not one with the
    deep.
Men, not gods, devised it. Men, not gods, must keep.
Men, not children, servants, or kinsfolk called from afar,
But each man born in the Island broke to the matter of war.
Soberly and by custom taken and trained for the same,
Each man born in the Island entered at youth to the game—
As it were almost cricket, not to be mastered in haste,
But after trial and labour, by temperance, living chaste.
As it were almost cricket—as it were even your play,
Weighed and pondered and worshipped, and practised day and
    day.
So ye shall bide sure-guarded when the restless lightnings
    wake
In the womb of the blotting war-cloud, and the pallid nations
    quake.
So, at the haggard trumpets, instant your soul shall leap
Forthright, accoutred, accepting—alert from the wells of sleep.
So at the threat ye shall summon—so at the need ye shall send
Men, not children or servants, tempered and taught to the end;
Cleansed of servile panic, slow to dread or despise,
Humble because of knowledge, mighty by sacrifice.

Let an ordinary line serve as a test of Kipling's workmanship. "Weighed and pondered and worshipped, and practised day and day": the single word that might feel like cant is deferred twice, until we know exactly what gravity it had for the author; and, as a grace note, "from day to day" and "day by day" are elided, with an unhackneyed vigor superior to both. For the rest Kipling's triumph seems complete. Where a phrase like "servile panic," with its faintly Augustan ring, is used at all it is used flexibly, beside a terse anglicism like "cleansed." The metaphor of "the game," on which the drama turns, is brought out by such quiet steps that it seems to have been looked at from all sides, before our assent is requested. "Trained for the game," says Kipling, and then "As it were almost cricket," and again, as we reflect uneasily on the words: "As it were almost cricket—as it were even your play." At the close war has become one of the things men live for, a thing that has all the seriousness of play.

The tenderness of this passage is unusual for Kipling, in its depth as well as its complication. For his affection is given to a corporate body, as distinct from the individuals who compose it; and yet, the quality of his words suggests a concern with the suffering of individuals. The confusion of feelings is so poignant that one would suppose him to have prepared for "The Islanders" through much of his work in the preceding years. In fact, only months before this poem, Kipling had made a popular success with a poem of almost an opposite tone, "The Absent-minded Beggar."

> He chucked his job and joined it—so the job before us all
>   Is to help the home that Tommy's left behind him!
> Duke's job—cook's job—gardener, baronet, groom,
>   Mews or palace or paper shop, there's someone gone
>   away!
> Each of 'em doing his country's work
>   (and who's to look after the room?)
> Pass the hat for your credit's sake,
>
>   and pay! pay! pay!

Was this meant for the same islanders? Certainly, the moral is altruistic rather than selfish, and so far in keeping with a Burkean high-mindedness. Yet it appeals to, and wants to foster, a native coarseness of temperament, according to which nothing need ever be changed. "Patch up everything you skipped," it seems to say, "but get on just as you are." The words were set to music by Arthur Sullivan.

It takes some ingenuity to trace the work of a single hand in these two poems. The difficulty will be more vivid if I add to the comparison still a third tone, "The odds are on the cheaper man," and a fourth:

> So the more we work and the less we talk the better results we
>   shall get.
> We have had an Imperial lesson. It may make us an Empire
>   yet.

With many other poets, a solution to the puzzle could invoke "the willing suspension of disbelief." This will not do for Kipling. Indeed, it would be truer to speak of an unwilling adoption of beliefs. Kipling's practice therefore sharpens the more general difficulty that I pointed to in his thinking about poetry. His rhetorical versatility makes him, once again, an unlooked-for double of the modernist, by producing the results associated with the ironic doctrine of "the mask." If the Victorian question remains—What was it like to be the author of all Kipling's utterances?—one thing only is plain. His poems offer themselves as *tests of authority:* of the degree of our loyalty to it, of what we feel when we hear its tones and what we feel when we speak them. Such gestures will seem to be implausible except where an author claims his audience's limitations as his own. But that is just what Kipling always does. The chance, however, for a next experiment is left to the author alone, who knows of other audiences and can imagine other gestures.

I prefer "gesture" to its synonyms because it is connected etymologically with "jest"—a word that carries a peculiar importance for Kipling. The easiest text to recall is "Zion":

> The Doorkeepers of Zion,
>   They do not always stand
> In helmet and whole armour,
>   With halberds in their hand;
> But, being sure of Zion,
>   And all her mysteries
> They rest awhile in Zion,
> Sit down and smile in Zion,
> Ay, even jest in Zion;
>   In Zion, at their ease.

The poem—though inscribed "1914–1918"—is among the happiest Kipling ever wrote about warriors. If, in this opening stanza, the word were not "jest" it would have to be "love," for it prefigures a communion in which all may "Sit down and sup in Zion— / Stand up and drink in Zion / Whatever cup in Zion / Is offered to our lips." What made Kipling put this kind of pressure on the word?

According to the *OED*, jest, which shares a root (*gesta*) with other words about exploits or doings, itself began by referring to the same class of things. A closely derived meaning was a tale, or narrative of exploits; so that the modern sense we take for granted occurs at a third remove: for us, it denotes the witty, sometimes mocking interruption which splits up the telling of a tale (but which in doing so may offer a fragmentary rival tale). The first citation to place "jest" as a merely antithetical expression—"a thing that is not serious or earnest"—comes from Gay in 1732: "Life is a jest, and all things shew it, / I thought so once, and now I know it." But there, we are still halfway between "Life is a joke" and the older "Life is a tale (told by an idiot)." Cowper takes it a step further, making the newer sense the primary one, but staying alert to the etymology for the sake of a compound that suggests antithetical *wisdom:* "The Scripture was his jest-book, whence he drew / Bon-mots to gall the Christian and the Jew." One may be reminded that Cowper was another party poet, though of a party opposed to Kipling's. At any rate, the 1885 "Prelude" to *Departmental Ditties*—a completely felt poem, written when Kipling was barely twenty—relies on a similar perspective that stops short of irony.

> I have eaten your bread and salt.
>> I have drunk your water and wine.
> The deaths ye died I have watched beside,
>> And the lives ye led were mine.
>
> Was there aught that I did not share
>> In vigil or toil or ease,—
> One joy or woe that I did not know,
>> Dear hearts across the seas?
>
> I have written the tale of our life
>> For a sheltered people's mirth
> In jesting guise—but ye are wise,
>> And ye know what the jest is worth.

Kipling here apologizes for what may seem to need no apology, the sharing of every action and passion with his characters.

But perhaps it is not altogether a sharing. Oscar Wilde said that Kipling was a great poet of vulgarity: "Dickens knew its clothes and its comedy. Mr. Kipling knows its essence and its seriousness." So Kipling may have felt a warrantable anxiety, lest in allowing outsiders to see the clothes of a life he be accused of betraying its essence. To judge by the poem, however, he had a more elusive sense of his role. He tells us only that there is a connection in his writings between a truthful bearing of witness and a watch kept *beside* a subject. He is a jester in that he stands apart from a storyteller who would identify with his hero effortlessly. At the same time, his attitude is only a "jesting guise"—not part of his disposition, but a security without which the tale would stay wrapped in earnest decencies. Kipling does not exempt himself from the jester's unhappy fate as a comic butt: one can see his acceptance of the role in a self-depreciating flippancy which sometimes brings his early poems to a premature close; and, much more, in his self-portrait in *Soldiers Three*, as the journalist whom the men can be easy with and blow the gaff, because they know his place is at the safe edge of things. All these qualifications give "jest" a special strength for the wise, and with the concluding line it turns into another name for truth.

One might say more conditionally that jest is truth, accommodated to an audience with whom the poet's relation is tactical, but ready for another audience with whom his relation may be moral. Good propaganda in Kipling's view—including much of the poetry he would have called great, and the prose he thought greatest, John Bunyan's—must seek to convert the first sort of audience into the second. He does not suppose once the task is accomplished, jest will have become unnecessary; on the contrary only then will it be fully intelligible: having ceased to be entertainment, it emerges as the part of experience that can be borne. In *Something of Myself*, Kipling avoids so exalted a conception of his powers, largely I think from the same modesty that keeps him from an irritable self-regard. Yet he does break with his reticence once, near the end of the book, in the chapter on "Working Tools."

> Let us now consider the Personal Daemon of Aristotle and others,
> of whom it has been truthfully written, though not published:—
>> This is the doom of the Makers—their Daemon lives
>>   in their pen.
>> If he be absent or sleeping, they are even as other men.
>> But if he be utterly present, and they swerve not from
>>   his behest,
>> The word that he gives shall continue, whether in
>>   earnest or jest.
>
> Most men, and some most unlikely, keep him under an alias
> which varies with their literacy or scientific attainments. Mine
> came to me early when I sat bewildered among other notions,
> and said: "Take this and no other." I obeyed and was rewarded.
> It was a tale . . . called "The Phantom Rickshaw." Some of it
> was weak, much was bad and out of key; but it was my first
> serious effort to think in another man's skin.
>
> After that I learned to lean upon him and recognize the sign
> of his approach.

To include the word he is willing to pay a visible cost, in the form of the quaint rhyme-word "behest."

But the passage is revealing for another reason as well. More plainly than any earlier moment of Kipling's writing, it declares that a liberty of invention which could be granted by the Daemon alone was to him inseparable from the act of sympathy. And his capacity for that act, the "attempt to think in another man's skin," he connects with the possibility of jest. This seems the place to observe that Kipling elsewhere can be very loosely idiomatic. Though always a careful writer, he is an early modernizer—using "transpire," for example, as an equivalent of "happen," and calling a wild fit of laughter "hysterics." In view of such habits one is all the more impressed by the passages—otherwise quite various in style—where he elects to use an old word in a sense that is fading. At intervals, he does present jest as a simple counter for "joke," and his motives are easy to see. It helps to legitimate the Stalky world—gives a Shakespearean panache to the disgusting adolescent prank. Yet after first noticing the word, I began to read with an eye for it, and an extraordinary number of his uses belong to the sense I have been citing.

Of the many other instances I choose one from *Kim* which echoes the 1885 "Prologue." Kim has already gone to St. Xavier's school, measured himself against the other Anglo-Indian boys for a term, and decided to run away for the summer. He intends to return after vacation; meanwhile, to make the escape he needs a disguise:

> He went out into the warm rain, smiling sinfully, and sought a certain house whose outside he had noted down some time before. . . .
>
> "Arre! Dost thou know what manner of women we be in this quarter? O shame!"
>
> "Was I born yesterday?" Kim squatted native fashion on the cushions of that upper room. "A little dye-stuff and three yards of cloth to help out a jest. Is it much to ask?"
>
> "Who is she? Thou art full young, as Sahibs go, for this devilry."

He tells her of an assignation with the daughter of a regimental schoolmaster—a lie based on her mistake—and proposes a disguise as a gardener's boy. The woman then completes the jest she has started: making him up for the role, dabbing his face with brown dye; and, when he complains of being unshaven, granting his wish even though it is not her trade.

> "All this disguise for one evening? Remember, the stuff does not wash away." She shook with laughter till her bracelets and anklets jingled. "But who is to pay me for this? Huneefa herself could not have given thee better stuff."
>
> "Trust in the Gods, my sister," said Kim gravely screwing his face round as the stain dried. "Besides, hast thou ever helped to paint a Sahib thus before?"

"Never indeed. But a jest is not money."

"It is worth much more."

"Child, thou art beyond all dispute the most shameless son of Shaitan that I have ever known to take up a poor girl's time with this play, and then to say: 'Is not the jest enough.' Thou will go very far in this world." She gave the dancing girls' salutation in mockery.

The encounter works up to a kind of ingratiation that Kipling was scrupulous to omit from the rest of *Kim*.

Of course any reader will feel charmed: by the boy's confidence, his adroitness and impudence; and by the impression that he is right to show these qualities, for he will go far. But the delighted marveling at "the most shameless son of Shaitan," followed by "the dancing girls' salutation," gives a prominence to the encounter that is in excess of the dramatic motive. The exchange lingers uneasily for another reason too. We have been aware throughout that Kipling *can* think in another man's skin, whether it is Kim or the lama or the British soldiers and missionaries. Now at this turn of the story, when Kim has proved to be adequately white, with the result that the effort to sympathize with him looks less remarkable—just at this point, Kim himself decides to put on another man's skin, literally: he is dyed brown to help him pass. From the perspective of melodrama it might simply appear that he has reverted to an earlier nature. But for Kipling a more solemn change has occurred. It is here for the first time that Kim justifies the affection of his author, by becoming like his author. And the drama is played out exclusively for those who know the code of the jest: "Ye know what it is worth." We are thus asked to share Kipling's own pleasure in his disguise as the wayward boy—a boy of secret good parentage, gifted with the impulsive sympathies of the author, who can compass all humanity by his sport. The recognition takes place through Kim's connivance yet without his knowledge, and therefore without spoiling him. I do not think it quite comes off: it has an air of wheedling with the reader behind the hero's back. Nevertheless, the scene gives a clue to the pathos Kipling invested in a book that modern critics have ranked highest among his works.

In his 1906 speech at the Royal Academy dinner, Kipling described the artist as the "masterless man," and this may be taken equally as a description of Kim. He is still a boy, just on his way to manhood, but, one feels, unmastered and certain to remain so. As one looks back at the story, however, he takes on a slightly different aspect. He is a serviceable boy, fond of obeying many masters provided his duty is also sport. Colonel Creighton (master of the "game"), the lama and Mahbub Ali (mentors of spiritual life and commerce respectively), all praise him in the style of Prospero's compliments to Ariel: "Bravely done!" Their words suit a character whose service is never in question. Doubtless to say this of Kim is not quite just—nothing one can say of him is—but the reason is not the subtlety of his moral life, but rather a confusion in Kipling's sense of him. Kim descends from a pair of nearly antithetical characters, Tom Sawyer and Huck Finn. The plot of the novel, indeed, is modeled on that of *Huckleberry Finn*—the lama is Nigger Jim— and it faithfully repeats the Tom Sawyer ending of *Huckleberry Finn*, with its elaborate practical jokes. But, partly because of this resemblance, I believe there is a promise in *Kim* that is not kept. We are led to expect that Kim will resemble Huck in the depth of his judgments of the grown-up world around him. But whereas for Huck the judgments come from himself and have a cost, for Kim they are one stage of a game whose rules he wants to learn in full. Some of his judgments do carry moral weight; but they always have a grown-up behind them. When he calls Mr. Bennett a fool, he is reporting the lama's opinion; when he puts paid to the spies, he does it on instruction from Hurree Babu; when he thinks that the talkative widow of the Hill Rajah is a tedious old proser, he follows a pattern of healthy revolt prescribed for boys by civilization. Even his escape from school is esteemed harmless by the usually suspicious Mahbub Ali: it is "the pony breaking out to play polo." Like Tom, and unlike Huck Finn, Kim breaks out of one game in order to play another.

Kim is therefore profoundly congenial with society just where Huck is dangerous to it; and though both novels deal with a rite of passage, *Huckleberry Finn* alone questions the authority that may control such a ritual: it affords neither a single pervasive tone, nor a decisive incident, to assure at last the worth of the game. In *Kim* by contrast, we are given the tone so steadily that we lose all concern for the incident, and are not disappointed when it fails to occur with much force. From a distance, the plot appears to require the coordination of two quests: one for a total knowledge of the codes of white India, the other for an unqualified acceptance of the vision of old India. But these quests are discrete from each other. The first begins with a memory planted in Kim at infancy, which fortune brings back when he can use it to join the game; the second he himself begins voluntarily, from an inward conviction of the lama's uniqueness; and the two coincide during the lama's pilgrimage in the Himalayas, where wisdom and counterintelligence may be pursued together. The moment of triumph for the game quest is the moment of defeat, hence of humility and the passage to true vision, for the lama's quest to be released from the wheel of things.

Let us try putting this another way. A jest (the trick that baffles the spies by coaxing their wicked designs into the open) leads to a truth (the lama's discovery of the connection between wickedness, self and the desire for revenge). On this view the jest that gives the story its final turn is a trial of both of the authorities that have set the plot in motion: the English police (who were right to entrust a delicate business to a novice) and the lama's faith (which lives up to its claim of dwelling apart from the world's business). The result is that both authorities are confirmed. We never learn to which of them Kim owes his first loyalty. But their coincidence is so lucky that it seems mean spirited to doubt he can satisfy both. Notice, however, that the jest is made anonymously. Kim works under cover in the last part of the story, his new identity guarded by his old friends the lama and Hurree Babu, just as earlier he was protected by the dancing girl's makeup. These are the only circumstances in which he can be sure of testing his powers without constraint. By now, the analogy between Kim and his maker ought to be clear. They are the hidden agents of a legitimate authority; and in its service they control, by feigning, all the personae of the life they witness. One might variously describe what they achieve by the sum of their inventions. A fair name for it, which Kipling himself was happy with, is empire.

Kipling's bias seems an unlikely one for a free mind to adopt. But, as one reads him, it feels consistent with his best qualities, among them an individual sense of duty and of compassion. His strengths are troubling because we have forgotten what imperialism could mean as an ideal. In his time it was not simply, what it has become simply, the exploitation for profit of a weaker people by a stronger one. A great power, now, in Africa or Latin America, means itinerant officers of multinational corporations, who supervise the projects of their company and think of the native population as either helpful or obstructive. Or else, it means the special forces of an interested government, who serve as advisers to a friendly militia, and encounter the native population as either subordinates or suspects. India gave Kipling a more complicated set of relations. It was possible in his time to associate imperialism with duty, with the long habitation of colonial and native races in a single region, and with a sort of knowledge that comes of responsibility. One may honor above Kipling those who saw that the oppressions of the imperial system made it finally wicked; but Kipling's was a position that could still be maintained without meanness and without self-deception.

The ideal was seldom realized even then. To speak of it eulogistically, however, did not seem merely delusive, any more than it did at the end of the eighteenth century. Here again Burke is an important figure. When he led the prosecution of Warren Hastings, the chief agent of the British East India Company, he argued that money itself was the corrupter of empire. The articles of impeachment against Hastings, accordingly, charged him not with failing to show a large profit, but with insulting human nature by the establishment of power for the sake of profits. To gain his private ends, Hastings made a routine practice of bribery, extortion and the petty stratagems of plunder: wherever he went to work, in the name of his company, he presided over the displacement of the local authorities and the eradication of the native culture. These Burke understood as abuses and for these Hastings was tried by the united lords and commons of England. A similar feeling for the morality of conquest became Kipling's natural inheritance, and may be traced not only in the teachings of his poems but in their incidental assumptions. They are expert in the implicit ways of giving a lesson half-learnt already. And so, very deftly, they call to mind the things that do not need to be taught.

As evidence of all the variety that the empire contains and ought to preserve, Kipling offers the many voices of his poetry. Their having been collected under a name, "Kipling," points to the vulgarity and the mystery of his calling, which turn out to be the same thing. Poetry since 1915 or so has not wished to be vulgar in his way. Yet Kipling's interest in empire seems to me another feature that marks him as a disturbing counterpart of the modernists, and not their antithesis. Modernism, too, was enthralled by the idea of empire, even if this was admitted in any number of sublimated versions, as the task of "saving civilization." That slogan, as Lucy McDiarmid has shown, appeared regularly in the postwar writings of Yeats and Eliot. Civilization meant above all the intuition of a past which ought to shape the present: an artist might invent, but always at the bidding of larger forces, compared to which his identity was nothing. To renew our awareness of his fate, he was even advised deliberately to hold himself at a distance. All this bears a contingent likeness to Kipling's practice, as the taboos of one culture may in principle repeat those of another, in spite of every disparity in the customs of marriage, worship and feeding the dead. The great difference that remains between Kipling and his successors has commonly been put down to the weaker gifts or the slighter seriousness of Kipling. My quotations all along have aimed at showing that this estimate is false. Rather, Kipling and the modernists addressed different habits of mind in their readers. The modernists won the battle. In time, people who knew how to read poetry stopped being people who knew how to read Kipling.

There is a quality of style by which a poet reveals that every word has been sounded to accord with his temperament. The audience of modern poetry may be defined as readers who have learned to listen for this—to hear a cadence, and know they hear the values that make it one poet's alone. Before the twentieth century, this was a property of certain poets, without respect to rank. Milton has it (not Shakespeare). Dryden has less of it than Pope, and Blake less than Coleridge. But modernism treated the presence of the quality as an index of poetic worth, and indeed as the defining trait of poetry as such. By this measure Yeats succeeds often; Eliot, often in his early work; and Kipling, at every phase of his career, fails utterly: he was toiling up the wrong path to art. Yet what modernism has taught us to care for need not be supposed a mark of a great soul. What is at stake is two attitudes toward speech, both of which are compatible with poetry, and both of which cannot exist in the same person at once. Yeats when he writes, "I have passed with a nod of the head / Or polite meaningless words," Eliot when he writes "The conscience of a blackened street / Impatient to assume the world," do not display finer sensibilities than Kipling. But they somehow evoke a reserve that he lacks. For, with a tact he could not possibly have admired, they imply an attitude of listening.

Eliot's terms of victory required him to say that poetry was naturally superior to rhetoric. The truth in his remark is that irony—an irony cleared of doctrine and emphasis—has proved easier to manage than jest. But there is a related contest from which I believe Kipling emerges more favorably. He cherished an ambition to recover the human types, from the high to the low, the refined to the grotesque and the fluent to the stammering, all with an ease which appeared to have passed away from poetry after Browning. Some such ambition may be granted also to the critic who wrote essays, close together, on Lancelot Andrewes and Marie Lloyd: but we read these, and they are meant to be read, as a wishful declaration of hopeless aims. Kipling, on the other hand, sat down and wrote "Sestina of the Tramp-Royal":

> It's like a book, I think, this bloomin' world,
> Which you can read and care for just so long,
> But presently you feel that you will die
> Unless you get the page you're reading done,
> An' turn another—likely not so good;
> But what you're after is to turn 'em all.

He is the poet, and almost the *man* of all who ever lived, to have made a sestina of the end words "long," "done," "world," "die," "good," "all."

Sometimes, as here, the possibilities that Kipling opens do belong to the common sentiments, and in that case a dramatic speaker detached from the author can explain them adequately. The larger possibilities of invention which concern him as well emerge only if one reflects on more than a poem or a story at a time. I have in mind everything that is suggested by a remark he makes at the end of "False Dawn." The story tells of a handsome young man who falls in love with the plainer of two English sisters in India. He accompanies both of them on a picnic excursion, and, in the confused darkness of a sandstorm, declares his love mistakenly to the prettier one; watches her become for some minutes the happiest girl on earth; but sends a male accomplice to retrieve the other sister, who has run out into the storm to console her grief. The story is told by the accomplice—anyone who knows Kipling can guess this—yet at the end it varies the sensational device that says, "The rest of what passed there cannot be told." We are informed instead: "There is a woman's version of this story, but it will never be written." It is odd how long one thinks about that; and it seems a good clue to Kipling's genius. For him, the reality of the other version, though it never can be told, is always what the jest was worth.

ELLIOT L. GILBERT

Silence and Survival in Kipling's Art and Life

*I have noticed in my long life that those who eternally break in on Those
Above with complaints and reports and bellowings and weepings are presently
sent for in haste, as our colonel used to send for slack-jawed, down-country
men who talked too much.*

—*Kim*, chap. 3

On September 27, 1915, Rudyard and Caroline Kipling's only son John
was reported missing in action in the Battle of Loos, just six weeks after his
eighteenth birthday. The young man seems to have been killed almost in-
stantly, but his parents had to endure two years of official silence about his
fate before they could definitively establish that John was dead. And it was
not until six years later still that the father was able to bring himself to break
his own silence about the event and allude directly and publicly to the loss
of his son. That allusion appears in his two-volume history, *The Irish Guards
in the Great War*, the dutiful record he compiled of the military unit with
which John had fought and died.

At that, the reference is extraordinarily reticent. Indeed, the single
mention of John in the book surely constitutes one of the strangest memorials
ever composed by a father for a beloved child. "Of the officers," Kipling
reports the casualties at Loos, the Guard's first experience under fire,

> 2nd Lieutenant Pakenham-Law had died of wounds; 2nd Lieu-
> tenants Clifford and Kipling were missing, Captain and Adjutant
> the Hon. T. E. Vesey, Captain Wynter, Lieutenant Stevens, and
> 2nd Lieutenants Sassoon and Grayson were wounded, the last

From *English Literature in Transition, 1880–1920* 29, no. 2 (1986). © 1986 by Elliot
L. Gilbert.

being blown up by a shell. It was a fair average for the day of a
debut, and taught them somewhat for their future guidance.

Elsie, the Kipling's only surviving child, was troubled by such reticence, by
her parents'—and particularly her father's—tendency to leave strong feelings
unexpressed. "The two great sorrows of their lives," she writes in her memoir, referring to the deaths of her sister Josephine and her brother John, "my
parents bore bravely and silently, perhaps too silently for their own good."
And Kipling, like Carlyle, another advocate of silence, appears to have paid
the price for his extraordinary suppression of feeling with the gastrointestinal
disorders that tormented him during the last two decades of his life.

It is possible, of course, to dismiss Kipling's silence about his deepest
paternal feelings as just one more example of proverbial English taciturnity
and self-control. (Kipling himself makes the pathos of such self-control—
specifically, of a mother's denial of her son—the theme of his W.W. I story,
"The Gardener.") But the British have long had alternate models of emotional—and, in particular, parental—behavior available to them. In no less
popular a work than *A Christmas Carol*, for example, Dickens, writing about
Tiny Tim's death, approvingly describes Bob Cratchit's strong emotional
response. "He broke down all at once," Dickens says of Bob's grieving for
his son, "he couldn't help it. If he could have helped it, he and his child
would have been farther apart perhaps than they were." One might argue
that the very appearance of this scene in the story shows that Dickens felt
it to be needed as a corrective to congenital English reticence, and that the
passage thus confirms the existence of that reticence as a national characteristic. But even granting the fact of such a characteristic, Kipling's suppression
of parental feeling, both in the passage from *The Irish Guards* and in private
life, continues to strike us as excessive, a curiously exaggerated—not to say
pathological—emotional anesthesia in which unhealthy silence substitutes
for a therapeutic expression of grief.

What makes this silence so notable is, of course, the fact that Kipling
was a writer, a man who believed that words are—as he put it himself—
"alive and walk up and down." Indeed, as David Stewart has persuasively
argued, Kipling was, both in his life and in his work, unusually attentive to
sound, having acquired an "oral-bilingualism" in part "from hearing his
mother and his *ayah* speak simultaneously." That experience is reflected again
and again in the preoccupation of so much of the verse and fiction—especially
the soldier stories and *Kim*—with dialect and transliteration. Stewart also
notes that "Kipling, his parents and sister read aloud to each other" and that
the young author "tested orally every poem and story he wrote."

To these points may be added the fact of Kipling's unusual "noisiness" as a boy; his maternal grandparents and other relatives describe him as having been more talkative and self-assertive than other Victorian children, a trait that was clearly responsible for much of the rejection and pain he suffered in the House of Desolation. It was also a trait that carried over into his fiction, helping to produce the raucousness and hysteria of many of the practical joke and revenge tales as well as the brash tone of the early writing in general. One of the principal objections of contemporary critics to *Plain Tales from the Hills*, for instance, was to the author/narrator's know-it-all manner, his officious "showing off." Stewart alludes to this characteristic of the early work when he speaks of Kipling's "precocity and cleverness," emphasizing what he calls the young writer's "willful deployment of language," a particularly apt phrase, as we shall see.

II

But despite the strong case that can be made for the primacy of sound in Kipling's life and art, it is possible to argue that the author was even more deeply committed to silence, not only in personal responses to experience like his stoicism about the lost children, his tendency toward reclusiveness, and his systematic destruction of manuscripts and correspondence, but also in his role as writer. In that authorial role, his concern—paradoxically—is again and again with depicting the level of reality that lies beyond the reach of language, and his principal technique involves one aspect or another of *aposiopesis*, the rhetorical tactic whose purpose is to withhold some final revelation. Significantly, he was at his best in brief works—lyrics and short stories rather than novels—works, indeed, that sometimes seem to be pruned past the point of intelligibility, to be so compressed, as C. S. Lewis puts it, that they are "not quite told." Lewis is alluding here to the famous passage from *Something of Myself* in which Kipling describes his unusual system for cutting a manuscript. "Take of well-ground Indian ink," the posthumous memoir instructs,

> as much as suffices and a camel-hair brush proportionate to the interspaces of your lines. In an auspicious hour, read your final draft and consider faithfully every paragraph, sentence and word, blacking out where requisite.

It is suggestive that in writing about his work, Kipling chose to wax mystical—using such terms as "auspicious" and "faithfully"—not about the *selecting* of words but rather about their *removal*, as if for him the whole secret of the storyteller's art lay in the avoidance of overt assertion. Hemingway, who much admired Kipling's craftsmanship, particularly praised the process described here for the way in which it allows what has been excised to persist in the work as a silent presence, defined by the ghostly shape it has left in the material that remains; and in fact this is the essence of Kipling's art, an art in which, as W. W. Robson has noted, the author "brought to its strange perfection [the] narrative manner of implication, abstention, and obliquity." If it is true, as has been remarked, that the rests in a Mozart composition are also by Mozart, the silences in a Kipling story are just as identifiably Kiplingesque, and it is often those silences that contain what the author most wishes to say.

Merely to list the works by Kipling that employ this technique would be impractical in a brief essay. Sometimes the obliqueness takes the form of a simple sleight-of-hand trick, as in "The Brushwood Boy," where a kiss, not directly described, is conveyed to the reader through the behavior of the lovers' horses. But more often the reticence and referentiality in a Kipling story are keys to the work's larger meaning. In "Mrs. Bathurst," for instance, several men try to piece together, from ill-assorted fragments of information, recent events in the life and death of a colleague, their account, in the end, remaining precisely as unintelligible as the behavior of their friend, whose last recorded words in the tale are "the rest is silence." "The Gardener," a late work that never directly puts its final insight into words, appropriately records the life of a woman who is unable to acknowledge her own son, even after his death. In "They," the auto circles down to the visionary garden of dead children, ghostly shapes left behind in the living world from which they have been excised, and the narrator finds that he can only hope to preserve the elusive meaning of the scene by permanently withdrawing from it. In "The Wish House," another of the obliquely told later stories, the effectiveness of the protagonist's sacrifice depends upon her allowing the beneficiary of her action to remain unaware of what she has done. And in a sardonic reversal of this theme, "Dayspring Mishandled" recounts an elaborate plan of revenge that must, at the last moment, be concealed from its victim. What Robson calls "the elliptical mode of narrative" of this last work has particularly troubled readers, but as the critic puts it, the story's "obscurities are appropriate in a tale which deals so much in the hidden springs of action." Yet the same might be said of each of Kipling's reticent stories; the indirection of their method is meant also to be thematic, serving the author's perennial vision of a world whose deepest truths are those that cannot be spoken.

But Kipling intends silence to serve still another purpose in his fiction,

and, ironically, it is in *Kim,* a book that contains some of his richest experiments with the recording of sound in print, that the celebration of silence
appears most explicitly. Throughout this novel of a young man's coming of
age, the rule of behavior most often emphasized is an injunction against
indiscriminate speech. "By Jove, O'Hara," Kim is lectured at one point by
Hurree Babu, his senior in the Secret Service, "I think there is a great deal
in you; but you must not become proud and you must not talk." The lesson
is one, however, that Kim seems hardly to need since earlier, in reply to
Mahbub Ali's question: "Why didst thou not tell before?" the boy had already
known enough to reply: "There is no need to tell more than is necessary at
any one time." Along the same lines, Creighton Sahib is approvingly presented by Kipling as, in the words of the story, "obviously respect[ing] people
who did not show themselves to be too clever" while in one of the book's
most memorable passages, the scene in which Kim succeeds in resisting the
hypnotic powers of Lurgan Sahib, Lurgan comments in astonishment: "You
are the first who ever saved himself. I wish I knew what it was that . . . But
you are right. You should not tell that—not even to me."

This last enjoining of silence is perhaps the most resonant of the many
in the book because it occurs in the context of a scene in which Kim is
presented as a kind of artist. "From time to time," Lurgan tells the boy,
"God causes men to be born—and thou art one of them—who have a lust
to go abroad at the risk of their lives and discover news." This is, of course,
an appropriate way to speak of a budding young Secret Service agent, but
there is more than a suggestion in the passage that Lurgan's words are
intended by the novelist as a comment on creative performance in general.
Certainly, Kipling would have described his own authorial activities as a
form of "going abroad to discover news," itself a life-risking business, as he
playfully points out in the 1906 after-dinner speech called "Literature" which
he delivered to the Royal Academy. In this characteristically brief talk,
Kipling introduces us to the aboriginal poet, the first man to succeed in
describing the world in language so powerful that his words "become alive
and walk up and down in the hearts of all his hearers." But such success,
we are told, terrifies the other members of the poet's tribe, who "seeing that
the words were certainly alive, and fearing lest the man with the words
would hand down untrue tales about them to their children, took and killed
him." The paradoxical point that Kipling seems to be making, both in this
passage and in the scene between Lurgan and Kim, is that, in a world where
language may too easily become the medium for "untrue tales," the survival
of an artist depends, to a very great extent, on his knowing when and how
to keep silent.

But the artist is not the only one whose survival depends on this knowledge. In another passage from *Kim*, the theme of the often lethal consequences of speech is presented in more universal terms. "I have noticed in my long life," says an old soldier early in the novel, "that those who eternally break in on Those Above with complaints and reports and bellowings and weepings are presently sent for in haste, as our colonel used to send for slack-jawed, down-country men who talked too much." At the political level, a passage like this presents Kipling at his least attractive, seemingly defending a naive ideal of *noblesse oblige* in which basic rights are for the strong to confer unasked rather than for the weak to demand. "My rights," Private Ortheris contemptuously snorts in a phrase that can be identified with, among other things, Kipling's well-known disapproval of trade unionism, "I ain't a recruity to go whinin' about my rights." Nor can the fact that Kipling shared this anti-democratic attitude with a number of his contemporaries—that Joseph Conrad, for example, takes essentially the same position in *The Nigger of the "Narcissus"*—be expected to rehabilitate this idea, as a political concept, for the modern reader.

But as a metaphysical insight, Kipling means us to understand, the statement by the old soldier in *Kim* is a perennial truth not governed by changes in social theory. What the old man is referring to when he speaks of "Those Above" (significantly, the two words are capitalized) is, of course, the powers that inform events, the forces that order the universe. It is these powers and forces, Kipling argues, that we should be careful not to attempt to importune or second-guess. For in the efforts we make to assure our survival by willfully shaping our own destinies, we are likely to be interfering with much more propitious arrangements, arrangements in which we ought to have been wise enough in the first place to acquiesce. Thus once again, it is silence that Kipling recommends here, silence as the best hope for survival in general and, as we noted before, as the best hope for the survival of the artist in particular.

III

To find at least one explanation for the unusual juxtaposition of silence, survival, and art in Kipling's life and work, it is necessary to turn to the much discussed and analyzed Southsea episode, young Rudyard's six-year sojourn at Lorne Lodge, the infamous "House of Desolation." What exactly may have happened to the boy during those years seems now to be a mystery beyond any possibility of final solution, but a few facts are not in doubt: the fact that at the age of six the young Kipling was suddenly and without explanation removed from the colorful world of Anglo-India and from the presence of doting parents and sent to live with strangers in the glum, evangelical atmosphere of an English provincial town; the fact that the noisy ebulliance that had so endeared him to his parents and servants now came to be redefined as a form of sinfulness, to be punished and suppressed; the fact that owing in part to his failing eyesight and in part to the Puritanism of his new guardians, he was soon brought to associate every manifestation of language—reading, writing, story-telling, speaking—with physical weakness, dishonesty, and his irredeemably fallen nature.

Our principal sources of information about the Lorne Lodge days are Kipling's own writings—"Baa, Baa, Black Sheep," *The Light That Failed*, and *Something of Myself*—and the corroboration of some of these records by Trix Kipling, the writer's sister, who shared the Southsea exile with him. What emerges from these documents, even when we have made due allowance for the unreliability of a child's memory and the exigencies of fiction, is the picture of a boy whose assertive creativity, taking the form of intellectual and, particularly, verbal precocity, was systematically condemned as—to use the disapproving Lorne Lodge term for it—"showing off." But "showing off" was itself a euphemism for a much stronger word, as the most famous of the Southsea incidents reveals. For having missed assignments at school because of his failing eyesight, and having concealed his plight from his guardians, Kipling was on at least one occasion made to walk about the streets of the town with a placard between his shoulders declaring him to be a "liar."

"Lying" and the somewhat less reprehensible "showing off," both linguistic acts, have in common manipulation of reality, the substitution of an invented—or at least of an embellished—world for the true one. The profoundest lesson Kipling learned at Southsea, the lesson that was literally beaten into him, was that language cannot be trusted as a vehicle for truth; that, as he was to put it later in his essay "Literature," "the man with words [can] hand down untrue tales." Certainly, the boy's own efforts at truth-telling were all too readily distorted into apparent falsehoods by his suspicious guardians, and in the end, his brutal treatment reduced him to the depravity of gloating over the ease with which such distortion could be achieved. "She says I'm a little liar when I don't tell lies," thinks Punch in "Baa, Baa, Black Sheep," "and now I do, she doesn't know." But if words can be the instruments of falsehood and lead to physical punishment, it must more than once have occurred to the young Rudyard that survival might lie in silence, that for one who seeks the truth, not language but rather the suppression of language is the best way of reaching the goal.

A number of critics have deplored the effects of such suppression on Kipling's life and work, arguing that the Southsea experience permanently damaged the writer, both as a human being and as an artist. Lord Birkenhead, for example, in what may constitute a bit of the amateur psychologizing that so offended Elsie Bambridge, speaks of the "morbid reticence in which [Kipling] was to shroud every secret corner of his mind from external scrutiny—in a constant, almost animal wariness and timidity, and an undying instinct for self-preservation." This view receives some support from a practicing psychiatrist, George H. Pollock, who sees the techniques Kipling developed for "mastering the tensions he endured in the house at Southsea" producing a lifelong "stoical resignation," a "persistent avoidance of introspection" that would explain, among other things, the blankness of his public response to his son's death. Angus Wilson too views Kipling's "exceptional reticence" as a negative element in his character, and Edmund Wilson extends this analysis to the writing, finding in Kipling's emotional anesthesia a form of denial that, in spite of—or perhaps because of—his experience with oppression at Lorne Lodge, left him prey to a species of silence the critic calls a "fundamental submissiveness to authority."

Such statements, even when they are exaggerated, have a good deal of truth in them, but it is important to remember that, as many of his most effective stories suggest, Kipling was himself well aware of the psychological and moral dangers of a too extreme withdrawal into silence. I have already mentioned "The Gardener," with its powerful analysis of the pathology of denial, its portrait of a woman whose silence, as one critic has remarked, "cuts her off from the human response she desires to make." But the same theme is developed at length as early as "Without Benefit of Clergy." In that work, published when the writer was still in his twenties, two lovers at first seek the illusory safety of isolation and reticence as a way of guarding their happiness, the woman declaring "We must make no protestation of delight, but go softly underneath the stars, lest God find us out." Such caution, however, such faith in the notion that if one is silent—that is to say, unobtrusive—one may not be noticed and punished, proves useless, and in the end, the couple agree to face down those same stars with a recklessness Kipling clearly admires. "There are not many happinesses," he writes, "so complete as those that are snatched under the shadow of the sword. . . . They sat together and laughed, calling each other openly by every pet name that could move the wrath of the gods." This is only one of the many works in which the author applauds a defiant response to those cruel gods who, as he puts it in "Baa, Baa, Black Sheep," "stand in the background and count the strokes of the cane."

Still, when Kipling came, in *Something of Myself*, to analyze the way in which the Southsea experience had prepared him for his life as a writer, he identified not self-assertion but "constant wariness" and "a certain reserve of demeanor" as the important lessons he had learned in the "House of Desolation." True, he also speaks, in his memoir, of the "lies he found it necessary to tell," describing them as the "foundation of literary effort." But in this he was merely being sardonic, for it was not falsehood but rather the defeating of falsehood by silence that would become the basis of his literary career. Indeed, one might argue that Kipling's single most creative act was to turn the reticence forced on him by his childhood agony into an instrument of personal and artistic survival, that his ultimate achievement was to press silence into the service of his best work as a writer.

IV

To understand how he managed to do this, we must often be willing to adopt a broad and somewhat unusual definition of silence, though of course there are instances when the subject of a work is silence in its most familiar sense. Of such instances, perhaps none is better known nor more cogent than the scene in *Stalky & Co.* in which the school is visited by a blatant super-patriot who preaches about the boys' duty to God and country and ostentatiously waves the flag. "In a raucous voice," says Kipling, "he cried aloud little matters, like the hope of Honour and the dream of Glory, that boys do not discuss even with their most intimate equals." Significantly, it is the noisiness of the speaker that is emphasized in this passage, his failure to understand that, as Steven Marcus has put it, "the values which inform [the moral life of the boys] are precisely those which are never to be explicitly referred to; like the true name of God, they are too sacred to be spoken." The principle here is an important one for understanding the metaphysical resonance that silence had for Kipling. All his life, perhaps as another consequence of the Southsea experience, the writer was engaged in a kind of ontological quest for what he often referred to as "things-as-they-are." Pollock reports, in his study of Kipling's abandonment, that deserted children are likely to become deeply concerned with "reality testing," especially with the relationship between reality and language. And indeed, one of the lessons Kipling tells us he learned in the House of Desolation was to note the "discrepancy between speech and action." It was a discrepancy that was to preoccupy him all his life, the gulf between "things-as-they-are" and those same things as mediated and inevitably distorted by language. Such distortion, a form of "showing off" or lie, is inevitable because, as Kipling saw and experienced it, language is by its nature nearly always more deeply obligated to the desires and expectations of the speaker than to the reality of what is being spoken of; it thus too often imposes its own order on the independent—and usually much more interesting—order of the world. One thinks, for example, of the anger of Findlayson, the chief engineer in "The Bridge-Builders," when months of work are destroyed at a blow because "the government of India, at the last moment, added two feet to the width of a bridge, under the impression that bridges were cut out of paper." A bridge has its own proper structure, Kipling indignantly reminds us here, and it is the business of all concerned with that structure to allow it to express itself in its own voice.

At his best the writer sought to implement this version of negative capability both in his own dealings with the world and in his art. Angus Wilson comments, for example, that Kipling "took part in children's games . . . not, as so many adults do, in order to impose his own shapes, but to follow and learn as well as to contribute." And the "multi-lingualism" that permitted the writer to talk to soldiers, scientists, men of action, people of many nationalities and backgrounds may be seen as one more form of the silence he adopted in order to allow others to speak. Thus the key to Kipling's fascination with dialect and shop talk is not his interest in sounds *per se* so much as his interest in sounds *other than his own*. I commented earlier on the appropriateness of David Stewart's phrase "the willful deployment of language" to characterize the brashness of the young Kipling. Stewart goes on to define the author's artistic maturity as precisely a function of his ability to relinquish mere personal control of his medium. "He gradually learned," the critic writes, "not so much to express himself as to suppress himself. His failures occurred when he interposed himself, tried to force language into willed forms and messages." Just as in "The Bull That Thought," then, where pain and death are movingly transmuted into art and life, so in Kipling's own career the suppression that blighted the Southsea experience became the creative principle of his best verse and fiction.

Such emphasis on self-abnegation and silence in Kipling's work took at least one highly controversial form, an insistence on the necessity of obedience. That the primary Law of the Jungle should be "Obey!" seems at first glance fully to justify Edmund Wilson's comment about Kipling's "fundamental submissiveness to authority," but the matter is more complex than that. The same Kipling, for example, who prided himself on his friendship with King George V refused to accept the Laureateship or any other official honor from him for fear of losing his independence as an artist. Thus, the obedience, the submission to authority Kipling counsels is not an indiscriminate one, and it can perhaps best be understood as one more form of silence. Those to be obeyed, Kipling argues, are those who demonstrably embody the authority of things-as-they-are, and who therefore speak with a voice truer and more powerful than one's own, before which it is right to remain silent. The best known instance in Kipling's own career of such obedience is his often recorded submission to what he called his "Daemon." About *Kim*, Lockwood Kipling is reported to have asked his son, "Did *It* stop or you?" and on being told that the novel had been completed under the aegis of the Daemon replied "Then it oughtn't to be too bad." Kipling himself codified the rule. "When your Daemon is in charge," he wrote, "do not try to think consciously. Drift, wait, and obey."

Those who take such advice run, of course, a grave risk: the risk of submitting to false authority, the risk of mistaking one's own voice for the voice of things-as-they-are; in more general terms, the risk of failure. But in Kipling's work, failure is often represented not as a defeat but as the necessary prelude to victory, a thesis insightfully developed by Robert L. Caserio in his essay "Kipling in the Light of Failure." Success is full of itself, confident, often obscuring, with its illusion of personal control, the larger independent forces that continue to move through things; in the "contract" he has signed with his Daemon, Kipling tells us, there is a clause requiring him never to "follow up 'a success' " lest he seem to be suggesting that he is now strong enough to dispense with assistance. Failure, on the other hand, has no choice but to acknowledge a power greater than itself, and this acknowledgement is its salvation, making of it a kind of *felix culpa*, the point, Kipling frequently argues, from which any truly important creative project must begin. "I have seen wonderful work done—with My Sword practically at people's throats," says the Angel of Death in the dark late story "Uncovenanted Mercies." One detects in such a passage the tone and atmosphere of Apocalypse, in which the failure—the silencing—of the entire material universe is required to reveal the greater spiritual reality that has always loomed behind it. And at the moment of the final revelation there is, appropriately, "a silence in heaven about the space of half an hour."

Underlying the passage from "Uncovenanted Mercies" is a characteristically unsentimental Kiplingesque definition of survival, one associated not with any glad superabundance of life (the swarming vitality and prodigious chatter of the Bandar-Log, for instance, are shown to be ephemeral and self-destructive) but rather with the grim *realpolitik* of "things-as-they-are." Especially for the older Kipling, survival means making do with what remains, with what little has managed to hold out against the merciless editorial processes of life. Certainly, *literary* survival is defined this way. "The magic of every word," Kipling writes,

> [must] be tried out to the uttermost by every means, fair or foul, that the mind of man can suggest. There is no room, and the world insists that there shall be no room, for pity, for mercy, for respect, for fear, or even for loyalty between man and his fellow-man, when the record of the Tribe comes to be written.
>
> ("Literature").

Such a ferocious and impersonal winnowing, not unlike that recommended in the passage on cutting a manuscript, moves language always in the direction of some final economy, fewer and fewer words being called upon to tell more and more truth until an ultimate truth is arrived at for which, in the nature of things, there can be no words.

Kipling was never in any doubt about the identity of that ultimate truth. In a world where the concept of "things-as-they-are" may itself be compromised by subjectivity and cultural relativism, the one reality that persists in the face of the most skeptical inquiry and beyond the most cynical manipulation of language is the reality of death. But that is also the one reality unreachable by language, as Kipling's response to his son's fate suggests; death is an editor who, in the end, blacks out every word and so necessarily reduces the literary artist who seriously pursues it to silence. Still, one who would survive as a literary artist (the image from "Uncovenanted Mercies" suggests) must be willing to press to the very brink of that silence, a procedure curiously symbolized by the woman in "The Wish House," whispering her request for death through a letter slot. The uncanny final sentence of *Something of Myself* makes the same point even more strikingly. "Left and right of the table were two big globes," Kipling writes, describing his study at Burwash, "on one of which a great airman had once outlined in white paint those air-routes in the East and Australia which were well in use before my death." It takes a moment for the mind to adjust to the point of view here, to the fact that the memoir ends with an assertion that it has already survived its author. Appropriately, the last word Kipling wrote for publication was "death," after which he discreetly withdrew into silence, leaving his books behind to speak with their own voices.

V

A discussion such as this raises once again the issue of Kipling's anomalous role in literary and cultural history, for it seems to identify him as partly a Victorian, partly a modernist, who makes largely uncategorizable responses to the problems he shared with other writers in both those periods. The fact, however, that we are here commemorating the fiftieth anniversary of his death—he died just a few days into 1936 and a few days after his seventieth birthday in late December 1935—points up a curious fact about his life that might help to account for the ambivalence of some of those responses.

People who are born, as Kipling was, in a year numbered sixty-five are so placed chronologically as to have their biblically allotted three-score-and-ten-year life spans exactly bisected by the turn of the century, and to be often a little uncertain, therefore, about which of the two centuries they ought to identify with. More imaginative people in this situation, especially literary people, are likely to have their whole experience colored by this fact, as, most famously, was Dante's, and in particular to think of the two halves of their lives as being—and perhaps even to act so as to cause them to be—radically discontinuous. Certainly, Kipling's life was full enough of striking discontinuities to encourage any apocalyptic fancies he might already have derived from his birth date, and to account for those two sides of his head for which he was so grateful. His first six years were spent with loving parents in the heaven of India, the second six with hostile strangers in the hell of Southsea, a hell from which he was suddenly and magically rescued by the return of his mother. In 1899 in New York, he played out before the whole world a dramatic scene of his own near-death and resurrection, a resurrection immediately shadowed by the death of his favorite child, and in 1902, he settled permanently in England. The clustering of these latter events around the turn of the century seems particularly notable.

In such a psychological context, the fact that it is impossible to place Kipling definitively as either a nineteenth- or a twentieth-century author (even the MLA Bibliography has over the years shifted him from one category to the other) may seem less puzzling. On the one hand, Kipling's grim sense of the human condition was a view he shared with many of his modernist contemporaries. Recording events of his early years, for example, he describes circumstances—abandonment by parents, punitive isolation, suspiciousness of religion, the gradual fragmenting and obscuring of the physical world through advancing blindness—which, if they had not been actual experiences, would seem textbook metaphors for modernist discontent. And one consequence of such experiences, we have seen, was to make of Kipling a writer who, in order to convey his vision of an alienating universe, employed techniques of fragmentation and obscurity that we also identify as distinctively modern. On the other hand, it is not really possible to speak of Kipling as a modernist author, largely because, in spite of the desperate childhood situation that shaped so many of his adult attitudes, he reaches, for his response, back to a kind of early romantic faith in immanence. We recall that in describing his method for cutting a manuscript, he advises that the task be undertaken in an "auspicious hour." But there can be no auspicious hour unless there are auspices, auspices defined by Kipling as a voice, independent of and wiser than our own, which may be invoked through a latter-day Keatsian "negative capability" or Wordsworthian "wise passiveness," both forms of silence.

There is a deep irony in the fact that one of the best known graphic images of Rudyard Kipling depicts him, in Max Beerbohm's wicked cartoon, with a tin horn in hand, cavorting noisily. For the truth about Kipling is, as we have seen, almost precisely the opposite. There was no aspect of his life and art—from biographical events to the philosophy he extracted from those events to the subject matter of his best stories and poems to the very structures of those works—that was not presided over by the profoundest silence. Randall Jarrell has remarked: "If I had to pick one writer to invent a conversation between an animal, a god, and a machine, it would be Kipling. To discover what, if they ever said, the dumb would say—this takes real imagination." Jarrell's comment, with its paradoxical play on the voices of the silent, is as shrewd as it is witty; even its slightly careless equating of "invention" and "discovery" as creative tools helps to make a point. Certainly, had Kipling been given Adam's denominative task in Eden, he would not have been such a "show-off" as to presume to name the animals. Instead, in an effort to "discover," not "invent," what the dumb would say, he would far more likely have asked each creature, as it passed, what it called *itself*. At such apocalyptic moments, Kipling believed, it is silence that reveals the deepest truth and produces the highest art.

ROBERT L. CASERIO

Kipling in the Light of Failure

The weakness . . . the wickedness . . . and the fat-headedness of deliberately trying to do work that will live, as they call it.

— *The Light That Failed*

We no sooner rediscover Kipling than we lose him once more. In every attempt at revaluation he is made to appear as a peculiar psychological or political case, to which his work is only subordinate. As a result he keeps escaping us, since we have yet to find terms in which to read not him but his writings, and we have yet to "place" his writings sensibly in a relevant literary tradition. Edmund Wilson and T. S. Eliot are responsible for this focus on the case rather than on the work; in spite of their sympathies, they make attention to Kipling's life or his "ideas" a necessary priority for reading him. Fortunately, the last quarter-century has provided good disinterested commentary on the writing itself by J. M. S. Tompkins and Elliot L. Gilbert, although only W. W. Robson's "Kipling's Later Stories" of 1963 and David Bromwich's "Kipling's Jest" of 1985 can stand as first-rate examples of scrutiny. If critics had read Andrew Rutherford's 1971 Penguin selection of the later stories with Robson in mind, we at last might have had an adequate revaluation of what Kipling wrote. But this did not happen. In the new Viking Portable Irving Howe's stirring comparison of Kipling's ideas about authority with Freud's is moving, but it is too loose an assignment of Kipling to our intellectual traditions, and Howe's conventional selections for the anthology may be a sign of the critic's greater interest in the psychoanalyst than in the writer. In spite of Howe, it remains as easy and acceptable as

From *Grand Street* 6, no. 1 (Fall 1986). © 1986 by Robert L. Caserio and Grand Street Publications, Inc.

ever for criticism to use Freud against "the Kipling case." Reviewing Alec McCowen's *Kipling*, a theatrical reading, John Simon insists that Kipling has no Freudian awareness of his own conflicts and contradictions—and that this is "a major cause of his not becoming a major writer." Simon insists on Kipling's "political and artistic reactionariness." And so it goes. It looks like the Kipling nobody read will always be Kipling whom nobody reads. Yet in the ironically perduring loss of Kipling there is an appositeness to his work. Critical insistence on Kipling's failure blinds criticism to the way its evaluations adhere to ideas about "success" that Kipling—and a significant Victorian literary tradition to which he belongs—calls into question.

Kipling's social thought or his ideas about art can not be understood without an analysis of his treatment of failure, especially as it appears in 1891 in his first novel, *The Light That Failed*. Now it happens that criticism has always judged the novel itself to be a failure. This judgment, I propose, has been based on unreliable, inadequately thought-out critical evaluation. As a result, the orthodox judgment has overlooked the power of the novel's thematic meditation on the meaning of success and failure in modern art and life. Kipling wrote the novel at a point in his career when a rigorous med-itation on success may virtually have imposed itself on him. Although in 1890, the year of the novel's composition, Kipling was only twenty-five, he had already produced two books of poems and three books of short stories. This work had grown out of his experience as a journalist in India since 1882; and the work's fame had preceded his arrival in 1889 in London, where throughout the next year he was lionized, with what seems to have been unprecedented adulatory attention. As if to attest to the merit of his celebrity, Kipling worked incessantly in 1890—worked so hard in fact that he brought himself to the point of emotional collapse. As it turned out, the novel that promised to crown his labors brought his reputation as well to the point of collapse. Now that in 1890 Kipling had chosen—for the first time, and at full length—to write about a world not foreign to his English contemporaries, about modern painters and English life, the critical tide turned. Having hailed him first as the Balzac of Anglo-Indian life, criticism said now that Kipling was more callow and self-indulgent than not, was brutal in thought and emotional quality, misogynistic, and, on the whole, ignorant of life. These epithets have stuck to the novel. In this way the critical tradition from the start obscured Kipling's treatment of success as an important subject throughout his writing; and it did so by an assertive, apparently infallible evaluative stance. And at the same time, the first evaluation of *The Light That Failed* got itself transferred to Kipling personally. What the short-sighted reviewers helped to establish as a fixed tradition was the image of Kipling as a person whose flaws were identical with those assertively assigned to *The Light That Failed*.

One possible reason for the short-sighted critical misreading of Kipling's novel is the lack of attention paid by the first reviewers to the literary tradition with which the novel seems to want connection. Swinburne and Swinburne's mid-Victorian reading of Blake, the entire Pre-Raphaelite legacy in fact—a legacy that for Kipling was a family matter, because of his close relation with his uncle, Edmund Burne-Jones—influences *The Light That Failed*. But before I open the case for this influence—or for at the very least the appositeness of the connection—it will be well to set out the novel's story of success and failure, and their modern motives. The novel's hero, Dick Heldar, is the 1880s equivalent of a photojournalist. During the British attempt to annex the Sudan, he is employed by a newspaper syndicate to draw pictures of scenes at the front. His pictures are good enough to gain the attention of London's art world, so that when he returns from the war he finds himself famous as an artist. Although he immediately sets up to practice art for art's sake, it is clear that Dick's success pleases him for reasons that are not aesthetic. We are shown that his choice of art as a vocation is the reflex of rancor from his orphaned childhood, when he was victimized by a sadistic legal guardian. His art and his success are indistinguishable from his need to take revenge for his early misery. Now Dick is in love with a childhood sweetheart, Maisie, another orphan and victim who is also an aspiring painter. Maisie too wants not just art but success and fame, and she believes that intimacy with Dick—let alone marriage—is too heavy a burden for her career. In courting Maisie, Dick derogates careerism and success, but even as he does so he is breaking up an affair between his journalist friend Torpenhow and a prostitute, Bessie, because he thinks the affair is damaging to Torpenhow's successful career. To revenge herself for Dick's interference in her attempt to "make it" by escaping the streets, Bessie destroys what may be Dick's masterpiece—a work he is painting as part of his virtually sadistic drive to succeed as Maisie's lover. But all these wars for success are doomed. Dick's career is coming to an abrupt end, because a head wound he suffered in the Sudan begins to make him go blind. Desperate to save themselves from the failure of their separate aims, the enemies Dick and Bessie briefly consider marrying each other; but by this point in the story Kipling has made it clear that success has an irreparably destructive dynamic. In the 1880s the British failed to conquer the Sudan, and at the end of the novel Dick returns to the scene of the imperialist failure. He finishes off his career by getting himself shot in a skirmish. In this suicide he exemplifies how, as the novel comes to suggest, the experience of loss of worldly ambition, and even death itself, are for the novel's characters more needful than anything else.

In its presentation of this story *The Light That Failed* is sensationally vivid and realistic. The immediacy and directness that is the effect of the writing is what we might expect only from the generation of writers after Kipling—from Lawrence or Hemingway. But the novel uses this effect not just for its own sake, but as an uncanny means to foreshorten (so to speak) an abstract, visionary analysis of an historical situation—of which its artist hero and heroine are representative. The novel presents its characters and their era as rooted in a terror of failure; and the motive for the terror is dramatized as an inordinately defensive response to loss—of love, of identity, of society, of life. All these losses are felt by Kipling's men and women to be in need of compensation; and since any form of success seems to deny vulnerability to loss and death, his characters make success a compensatory protective fetish. In the absence of any coherent religious or institutional address to death, Kipling suggests, modern failure—especially in love and in work—is a personal death, as if it were a likeness of the ultimate loss and vulnerability that are to be shunned and denied. Kipling's novel records a world and an era in which failure and death alike have become, as it were, unacceptable.

The typical psyches of the English world are thus exhibited in the novel as forms of counterviolence that use success to master failure, loss, and death. Perhaps surprisingly, Kipling points out both artistic creativity and psychosexual differentiation as two symptoms of the attempt at mastery. His artists, Dick and Maisie, make art and make love as enraged strategies in a battle for control over failure. Because each thinks the other has this control, both Dick's and Maisie's war and their artistic creativity are rooted in jealousy, which appears in *The Light That Failed* in every human phenomenon and which further produces or creates a spectrum of defenses against vulnerability. For Kipling, the worldly struggle to dominate loss has overtaken biology. Human sexual differentiation has become one of the defensive products of each sex's jealousy over the other's imaginary domination of death. The struggle between Dick and Maisie is a culturally determined combative difference of male and female, which creates an illusion of something jealously to struggle *for*, something jealously *to* dominate. But this struggle between the sexes which has come to define the sexes is only a diversion of their undifferentiated vulnerability to death. The counterviolence intended to master death makes impossible any love that is not a power struggle, not a secondary form of aggressive defense against loss. Love that may arise out of this struggle Kipling sees as only a mask for sadistic pity, for kindness or care felt by aggressors for their victims.

The historical world out of which Kipling writes is thus a totalized order of fruitless creative jealousy, which the novel exhibits in order to criticize. But it does more than criticize; it gestures towards a possible though grim road toward liberation: radical submission of "creative" human affairs to death. In making this gesture, the novel criticizes all its agents, not just Dick and Maisie but Kipling too. As a form attempting to portray the world the novel must exhibit itself, its writer, and writing in general as modes of failing light. As we shall see, Kipling even includes in the ending of the novel a self-reflexive moment that humbles the representational vividness from which his style derives its strength. Because the novel's and the novelist's own ambitions to ease the burden of mortality or to be enlightening about what lies beyond creative jealousy must avoid indulging the impulse to master failure and death, the visionary content of *The Light That Failed* suggests an ultimate, necessary rubbing out of its own power to act as a world-portraying canvass.

Perhaps only a twenty-five-year-old youth could assume and argue so abstract and comprehensive a pessimism about the world and about the place of creativity—whether aesthetic or sexual—in it. I think that a revaluation and recovery of this pessimism and the Victorian imaginations that are behind it might have a special current value. The thought is certainly in contrast to John Simon's gnashing of teeth over Alec McCowen's *Kipling:* "What purpose does it serve?" he asks—especially in America; what purpose will any revaluation of Kipling and his tradition serve, one might add, if the revaluation is not to be just academic? The question deserves an immediate response. Recovering Kipling and his tradition may justify itself to begin with if I briefly consider a kind of literary and political writing about failure that is closer to home and that indeed is, although without any acknowledgment, influenced by Kipling.

The Light That Failed, because it is about English war correspondents in the Sudan a century ago, gave writers from Stephen Crane on—Hemingway, Orwell, and Norman Mailer among them—the possibility of an alliance between war journalism and literary art. In its development this alliance has produced a body of work that has continued to focus on versions of Dick Heldar, versions of a failing or failed hero at odds with the battle for success being waged around him and within him. The most recent American product of this alliance grows out of American combat in Vietnam; and the acclaim in 1977 given to Michael Herr's *Dispatches*, a book about special correspondents in the war, might have been more cogent had it mentioned Kipling. The interest of Herr's book lies in a direction predicted by *The Light That Failed*. *Dispatches* suggests a need to live on the brink of personal and public failure and loss, without defensive denial of them. Yet this need for a radical lapse from—or liberation from—success can scarcely be admitted by American traditions, although the denial is costly. As C. Vann Woodward long ago pointed out, the South had an advantage in suffering defeat in the Civil War: it experienced the failure which every historical people has suffered, but which the United States has made unacceptable even to admit as a national experience. Herr's attachment to Vietnam is probably due to its having freed him from "success," to its having enabled him to breathe the un-American air of mortal vulnerability. In contrast to the soldiers, Herr and his fellow correspondents chose to live in death's shadow—a choice both full of fear and fearless, both vulnerable and defenselessly careless about life. This liberation from the fear of loss without any shirking of the fact of loss is what Kipling moves Dick Heldar towards, and what seems to have moved Herr to write *Dispatches*. But whereas Kipling shows the subversion of his hero's attachments to the social and sexual order and to art's place in both, in a way that analyzes the historical order as the reflex of a culture-wide terror of loss and death, Herr is cut off from such analysis. As a result, his book seems merely confused about the role failure and death play in his experience. Herr says "the press . . . never found a way to report meaningfully about death, which of course is what it was all about," but he goes on to say that he finally had to stop his observation of the war for reasons he can only cloud over. "We came to fear something more complicated than death, an annihilation less final but more complete, and we got out. . . . If you stayed too long you became one of those poor bastards who had to have a war on all the time"—presumably because the "something more complicated than death" *insists* on generating war "all the time." In Kipling's light Herr might have seen that it is the modern state's order of jealousy which has become the thing more complicated than death, that this order relentlessly and ironically generates war as the way to succeed against death, indeed against any vulnerability. Instead of making an analysis, Herr refuses explanation and suddenly turns his narrative into a success story. "All right, yes, it had been a groove being a war correspondent, hanging out with the grunts and getting close to the war, touching it, losing yourself in it and trying yourself against it. I had always wanted that, never mind why . . . I'd done it. [There] had always been marines or soldiers who would tell me . . . *You're all right man . . . you got balls*." The courage to be "all right" connotes the surmounting of death, and the success story turns out to be vulgarly male and vulgarly American. America lost, but the special correspondents did not. Nevertheless, against the success of rigorous male "fearlessness" in *Dispatches* one might set—more clearly than Herr finally does— the attractiveness his book assigns even if incoherently to a vulnerability that no "balls" can succeed against. It seems to have been *The Light That Failed*'s intention to make the case for such vulnerability, as the only escape from the historical and social state's way of having become the thing that must have a war on all the time.

The immediate purpose a revaluation of Kipling might serve, then, has to do with the historical relevance for an American context of the "moral" of failure suggested by *The Light That Failed*. This "moral" is that no ideology, no public purposes or wars, and no private "success" can negate mortality in any but a factitious and injurious way—though the way may be the path of shining worldly accomplishment—even of accomplishment in art. Artistic creativity, *The Light That Failed* asserts, cannot be separated out from the worldly aggressions that are produced by the attempt to master all loss. But this assertion is not merely young Kipling's. Having sketched an immediate American purpose to be served by thinking again about Kipling, I turn to the way Kipling's early vision must be tied to Blake's and Swinburne's role in Kipling's environment. It will be easier to contradict and to move beyond the traditional complaints about the novel once the literary sources that influence or at least coincide with Kipling's drama have been suggested.

To those who cherish the received ideas about Kipling, Blake and Swinburne—Blake especially—will seem too removed from Kipling for serious connection with him. Yet Eliot persistently couples Kipling and Swinburne, since Kipling's poems are full of Swinburne's rhythms and diction; and Dick Heldar's sketchbook—which belongs to the days before Yeats's edition of Blake, when the latter was virtually a Pre-Raphaelite possession, interpreted by Swinburne's pioneering *William Blake* (1868)—contains drawings of a model to whom Dick exclaims "What a fortune you would have been to Blake!" Of course I am hypothesizing influence, not documenting it; but environing influences of this kind, or at the very least the possible coinciding of these strong poetic imaginations produced by romanticism, must be allowed a major place in any speculative biography of Kipling's work. Kipling's immediate personal relations have been fair game for his interpreters; but for any author the writings and the writers he admires are no less live or personal than the author's parents, siblings, or children. The biographical treatment of *The Light That Failed* has analyzed the novel as a merely personal, literal family matter. Kipling was born in Bombay of Anglo-Indian parents, and he experienced the disturbing but customary fate of Anglo-Indian children: just before he was six, he and his young sister Trix were sent back to England and separated from their parents, so as to receive an English education at home. Ironically, "home" meant boarding in the house of strangers, with a retired naval officer and his wife in Southsea. Kipling's parents made a poor choice of guardians: the officer's wife was viciously repressive, and the house's educational order of the day was caning. Hence Dick Heldar's victimized childhood in *The Light That Failed* is autobiographical; and Maisie turns out to be a composite of Trix and another young woman, Flo Garrard, who came later to live in the same boarding establishment. In the analysis of Kipling's response to this experience, it has become conventional to say that it explains his alleged bent for coarseness and bullying, which he adopted as a defensive imitation of the canings; and that it made him hate women. His misogyny resulted from feeling betrayed and abandoned by his mother; and because Trix was treated better by the foster family than Kipling was, he felt enviously inferior to the sex that betrayed him. Now there is no reason to reject this biographical hypothesis; but since it is an hypothesis, it is at least questionable, and not a fact. My alternative hypothesis is that in the Burne-Jones household—during what Kipling himself called paradise-like vacations from Southsea—he early on became exposed to a literary culture which provided his precocious mind with a way to make sense of his misery that is as good as if not better than our psychologistic way to make sense of it. Burne-Jones was Swinburne's intimate, to whom the poet dedicated the notorious *Poems and Ballads* of 1866; his family was continually together with the Robert Brownings and the William Morrises; the Burne-Jones, Morris, and Kipling children published a family literary magazine. Kipling left Southsea in 1876 for school at the United Services College in Cornwall, where the headmaster who devotedly stimulated the boy's literary ambition was Cormell Price. Price was a schoolmate of Burne-Jones, a close friend of D. G. Rossetti, and had been one of the painters of the famous Pre-Raphaelite frescoes at the Oxford Union. So it is surely arguable that Kipling grew up saturated in Pre-Raphaelite culture, whose greatest poet was Swinburne and one of whose saints of art had been Blake. The biography of Kipling by Lord Birkenhead describes Kipling's celebrity in London in 1890 in terms that starkly contrast Kipling with Wilde, Beardsley, and the aesthetes, themselves the cultural offspring of Pre-Raphaelitism. But C. E. Carrington's biography keeps closer to the truth. At school, he tells us, Kipling "was a rebel and a progressive which is to say, in 1882—paradoxically—that he was a decadent. His friends, his teachers, were liberals, his tastes were 'aesthetic.' " It is scarcely credible that the young man who returned to London—and to the Burne-Joneses—in 1889 had cut himself away from his literary origins.

So it is arguable that at the end of *The Light That Failed*, when Dick Heldar divests himself of his identity and his art, in a blind surrender to the hazard and obscurity of death, Kipling's portrait of the artist as a young man follows the events central to Blake's portrait of the blind artist Milton. It is also arguable that Kipling insists on Dick's submission of his creativity to death's dominion because Swinburne's reading of Blake presents Blake as in fact a critic of artistic creation or generativity—as indeed a proponent of the failure of creation. Surprising though it may be, Swinburne enlists Blake in the cause of art for art's sake just because Swinburne sees Blake as an antagonist of creative power. For Swinburne, Blake is a consummate aesthete because he failed at worldly success, because he failed to attach art to any ulterior worldly purpose. He did so, according to Swinburne, because Blake cared not for creation but for salvation—and for Blake salvation was liberty, even liberty from the world. This radical freedom meant liberty from "the Creator's power" and from "the creative daemon," both of which rule the world as an order of creative jealousy. "The creative daemon," Swinburne says in one of his summaries of Blake's ideas, has "power . . . which began with birth" and "must end with death; upon the perfect and eternal man he had not power till he had created the earthly life to bring man into subjection, and shall not have power upon him again any more when he is once resumed by death." So death is the way of release: "where the Creator's power ends there begins the Saviour's power"; and Swinburne goes on to note that "confusion of the Creator with the Saviour was to Blake the main rock of offense in all religious systems less mystic than his own." Now the creative daemon in Swinburne and to some extent in Blake is both the Judeo-Christian God and the poet-god, the creator Milton for example, whose salvation will come in the yielding of his pride of life and art to a resumption by death. Not identifying his own work with such daemonism Blake is said by Swinburne to believe "all form and all instinct is sacred; but no invention or device of man's"; and for the same reason Blake is said to have assigned his books to "inspiration" and to "no invention"—because Blake believed, Swinburne says, that the "inlets and channels of communication [are] now destroyed by the creative demon." But although the fabrications of this demon-daemon have become the order of things, Blake is far from passive in response. Swinburne emphasizes Blake's destructive "ardour of rebellion and strenuous battle" against the Creator, against His inhibitings of liberty. "The God of nature . . . must have the organ of destruction and division, by which alone he lives and has ability to beget, cut off from him with the sharpest edge of flint that rebellious hands can whet."

This castration of the Creator practiced by the artist suggests the artist's self-violation in turn, insofar as he too is a generative god, whose creation of words and worlds by articulation's divisions must fall victim to his own war of liberation from articulation itself. No wonder Blake became what

Swinburne—in a way surely attractive to Kipling—describes as "full of the vast proportion and formless fervour of Hindoo legends." It is by becoming formless and inarticulate, by destroying the rational divisions and articulations of the Creator, that Blake practices art for art's sake—and for failure's sake. As Swinburne represents Blake's art, it is a mode of obscurity and darkness because it deliberately cultivates the loss of the world. The loss has no compensation. Accordingly, when Swinburne summarizes *Milton*, he neither mentions nor quotes the ecstatic hymning of imagination that in the poem follows Milton's liberation from selfhood. If the selfhood articulated by the creative daemon must fail, Swinburne thereby suggests, that failure must be the sole object of our attention and our advocacy. In Dick Heldar's career Kipling writes another version of Swinburne's suggestion, inspired by Blake.

The source of Blake's animus against the Creator-figure is the dynamics of the human terror of loss, with its consequent ironically destructive psychic and sexual defenses against that terror. What Kipling draws in Dick and Maisie was earlier drawn by Blake in Los and Enitharmon, especially in the initial sections of *Vala; or The Four Zoas*. A few points in those sections will be seen to bear on *The Light That Failed*. In *Vala*, "Tharmas, Parent pow'r" identifies his and Enion's daughter, "the infant joy" Enitharmon, with "Everlasting brooding Melancholy" because the child breeds fear in the parent that the love of the parents for each other will be lost to the child. This fear of loss gives birth to just the loss that is feared, so that a new infant, Los, is engendered. The infant's name keeps in play the idea of creative generation as a diminution of being, as itself a fall. Moreover Los's name stands for the loss that produces creative daemonism if loss is defended against rather than submitted to. Yet the children of the parent powers will not submit any more than their parents do. Reproducing in themselves their parents' terror of loss, the children compensate for their fears by regenerating themselves as agents of deceit, jealousy, and aggression. "If we grateful prove," Enitharmon tells Los, "they [the parents] will withhold sweet love, whose food is thorns and bitter roots." Thus the children seek to coerce love by bringing bitterness to their parents and then to each other. "Strong vibrations of fierce jealousy" make the children struggle to dominate each other, as a way to master the vulnerability in their mutual need. When Enitharmon smites the "sphery harp" to sing "a song of Death / It is a Song of Vala!"—Blake's very own poem—she is perpetuating a "rapturous delusive trance" whereby she can dominate Los. Blake here identifies his own art-song with a delusive, defensive strike against loss, with a beating or hammering that is a defense against vulnerability. But the exertion of the hammer is always the very loss it tries to drive away. Recognizing Enitharmon's coercive design, Los retaliates by striking her down, literally hammering his sister. Then he feels pity and contrite repentance for his jealous rage and fear—and calls it love. The result is a wedding of the two young artists, but they sit down to the wedding feast "in discontent and scorn." The desire to dominate vulnerability, to succeed against every weakness and dependency, creates an institution of love that is only the veil of a struggle. As Blake tells us in *Jerusalem*, in another attack on creativity, "Vala would never have sought and loved Albion/ If she had not sought to destroy Jerusalem; such is that false / And generating love, a pretense of love to destroy love." It comes to seem as if the pretense of love to destroy love is the origin of sexual differentiation, a point Swinburne emphasizes when he speaks—concerning *The Gates of Paradise*—of Blake's idea that humanity was "neither good nor evil in the eternal life before this generated existence; male and female, who from of old was neither female nor male, but perfect . . . without division of flesh." So, Swinburne comments, from "the separation of the sexes come jealous love and personal desire, that set itself [*sic*] against the mystical frankness of fraternity."

Now Kipling may not have known *Vala; or the Four Zoas* because Swinburne himself did not tackle the poem when he was in his twenties; Swinburne seems not to have read it even in 1906, when he comments on Yeats's edition. And after *Vala*, Blake softens his picture of Los and Enitharmon, to make them out as figures of mercy more than as harsh representatives of the order of creative jealousy. Yet there is an uncanny way in which Swinburne after all did "read" the *Vala* and did hand on to Kipling an accurate version of Blake's unsoftened picture of the brother-sister daemons. With penetrating ability to complete—in the form of his own work—whatever aspect of Blake's mythology was not available to him, in *Atalanta in Calydon* and in *Poems and Ballads* Swinburne imagines psychosexual fables that reproduce the struggles of Enitharmon and Los to dominate loss by "creative" jealousy. In *Atalanta* (which Kipling in his schooldays knew by heart) Althaea's fear of the loss of her son becomes a defensive, death-dealing aggression; her parent power, maternally jealous of Atalanta, comes to abet the paternal God whom the chorus curses as "The supreme evil" because he has created humanity as slaves to his jealousy. In *The Triumph of Time* in *Poems and Ballads* Swinburne turns away from the generative mother to a different maternal power, the sea—a liberator from the order of creative jealousy in which Eros too is trapped: "Death is the worst that comes of thee: / Thou art fed with our dead, O mother, O sea / But when hast thou fed on our hearts?" The sea promises a redemptive resumption by death, a liberating careless violence, that makes even suicide appear better than the human order instigated by fear of mortality.

Los and Enitharmon, and Swinburne's muse of liberating suicide—the mothering sea—reappear in the opening chapters of *The Light That Failed*. We might try now to see what specific help Blake and Swinburne contribute to a reevaluative reading of *The Light That Failed*. The standard reading, which needs to be set aside if we read Kipling's work on its own merit and yet with the antecedent poets in mind, is recirculated in Angus Wilson's opinions of 1978: the novel is "a farrago . . . of misogyny and false heroics and self pity"; the misogyny shows itself as male "wounds received in contact with the deadly other sex"; and "to balance all this misogyny," Wilson says, "we have the idealized world of men's men." It takes only ordinarily prejudiced inattention to make the facts of Kipling's plot fit this evaluation. We can say that Dick Heldar is destroyed by two women; by Maisie, who is frigid; and by Bessie Broke, who is a whore: the former breaks his heart, the latter destroys his last and greatest painting. In this misogynistic light the blindness Dick suffers can be read as Kipling's barely disguised fantasy of castration by women. Presenting its hero as a victim of this castration, the novel arguably rebukes women for trying to share the male's creative prerogatives. To support this standard reading what has been enlisted along with the facts of Kipling's childhood is the content of the novel's first, second, and fourth chapters, and their style—a striking, peculiar style that experiments with prose exposition as a form of rhyme. The first two chapters put back to back a first love-scene between the young adolescents Dick and Maisie—a scene in which they exchange kisses during a seaside pistol-shooting practice—and a war scene, much later in time, in which Dick suffers the head injury that will cause his eventual blindness. It is especially the rhyme of elements in both scenes that has led to the interpreter's connection of Maisie with aggression against Dick. In the first chapter Maisie misfires the revolver and sends gunpowder into Dick's eyes; when she then kisses Dick, the kiss on his cheek "stung more than gunpowder"; and after the kiss Dick's own aim with the gun is spoiled when Maisie's hair blows across his face. In the next chapter, as Dick in the Sudan is caught in literal gunfire, the momentary blindings of the episode with Maisie are echoed, in phrases that virtually quote the first chapter. Then in the fourth chapter once again the same phrases accompany the first reunion of Maisie and Dick since chapter 1. Moreover, in each moment of blindness Dick hears something like "Get away, you beast"—this command in the first chapter is from the children to their pet goat; in the second, from a wounded soldier to an attacker; in the third from a woman passerby on London Bridge to her lover. This "rhyme" has been taken by critics as Kipling's clinching equation of sexuality with bestiality—an equation necessary for any reading of the novel that identifies the female with the ultimate brutality, that sees her as a double (in the novel) for the most brutal aggressor, death.

But if we allow the possibility that Kipling, in the tradition of Swinburne and Swinburne's Blake, is not prosecuting one of the sexes, but is dramatizing a human order in which "jealous love and personal desire" have created the frightened separation of male and female and have set them both against each other, then the novel's opening, in all of its aspects, is not open to the customary dismissive reading. Like *Vala* or *Atalanta in Calydon*, the first chapter of *The Light That Failed* presents a compact vision of a world in which order is the creation of jealous agents, whose aim is to master the terrifying loss of love and life by successfully striking at or beating vulnerability whenever it is manifested. In this world the orphans Dick and Maisie are a fledgling Los and Enitharmon who respond to the threat of loss by becoming creator-sadists. This development makes them mimics of the parent powers whose own defensive response to loss is tragically regenerated by the children. In the novel's first chapter, Dick and Maisie have secretly purchased a revolver as a recourse against the beatings they receive from Mrs. Jennett, "the guardian who was incorrectly supposed to stand in the place of a mother to these two." Yet the beatings come from the mother only because, like Althaea in relation to the Supreme Evil, the female's sadism copies the male's. Dick receives "the average canings of a public school—about three times a month" and this "filled him with contempt [for Mrs. Jennett's] powers" to cane him. It fills him with contempt as well for the supreme caner, the male God. Dick's "home-training," as Mrs. Jennett calls her punishments, are inspired by her "religion manufactured in the main by her own intelligence and a keen study of the Scriptures. At such times as she herself was not personally displeased with Dick, she left him to understand that he had a heavy account to settle with his Creator; wherefore Dick learned to loathe his God as intensely as he loathed Mrs. Jennett." But although this loathing promises a revolutionary attack on the punitive Creator, Kipling shows how the attack is not executed because the movement towards liberation is overwhelmed by the fear of loss. Revolution is thereby diverted and the revolutionist becomes a copy of the oppressor. Mrs. Jennett herself, "anxious to remarry" because widowhood has made her an orphan of sorts, has turned the fear of what she has lost in life or will continue to lose into thorns and bitter roots, into the mastering of her dependents by beating them. And at the very moment in which the children play at killing Mrs. Jennett and her Creator they are frightened into continuing the order of beatings rather than liberating themselves from them. Realizing that they are about to lose each other (because Maisie just now announces that she is of age to leave her guardian), Dick's first and only recourse is to think of worldly vocation. His life's work will be a substitute for her—but it can be so, only if it will also be a success. But what can Dick succeed at? " 'I don't seem to be able to pass any exams;

but I can make awful caricatures of the masters.' 'Be an artist, then,' said Maisie," who has decided to become an artist herself. Art is the perfect calling for resentment: it caricatures the masters, and yet also reproduces them. Kipling's idea is that in a world ordered by offensive and defensive aggressions, art is no alternative to them. The imperialist caning of the Sudanese will be the arena in which appropriately Dick's art comes into its own. The violence Dick and Maisie are rehearsing in the first chapter thus passes into creativity itself; and their terror of the loss of love and power seals them into an aggression that becomes fatal competition with each other.

Although *The Light That Failed* as we shall see will go on to endorse a form of violence that is not terrified and defensive, Kipling is not endorsing the violence that the children use the revolver—and their choice of life's work—to implement. The signal to the reader not to endorse Dick closes the first chapter in the form of a dream that condenses the Blakeian and Swinburnian vision of loss-inspired creative aggression and psychosexual division. On the night of the shooting-practice Dick dreams he "had won all the world and brought it to Maisie in a cartridge box, but she turned it over with her foot, and, instead of saying, 'Thank you,' cried—'Where is the grass collar you promised for Amomma? Oh, how selfish you are!' " The cartridge box enclosing the world makes the world ammunition for the revolver. This detail is accurately analytic and foretells the truth. Dick's creativity will be a resentful stockpiling of aggressions; the success he will achieve will not be a matter of artistic "quality" but of his power of menace. Of course Kipling's point here is not concerned just with Dick; in the world he portrays, all the talk about art's achievement will be a mask for the competitive buildup of jealous power. Blake the visionary escaped the practice of art as ballistics because he was blind to the world and so to "success." Dick's dream tells us that he is not yet blind enough—he is too much of a worldling. The dream masks his own recognition of the terror of loss that motivates his world-beating. In *this* blindness he scapegoats Maisie: supposedly *she* is selfish, because she thinks Amomma, her pet goat, is worth more than the world Dick wins for her. But of course the blame attached here to Maisie keeps Dick from seeing anything clearly about himself.

What the reader can see clearly about both Dick and Maisie is concentrated in Kipling's use of Amomma in the dream and in the pistol-practice. The goat has eaten some of the cartridges, and the children become terrified that the goat will explode. Trying to drive the animal away "because he might blow up at any time," Maisie exclaims to Amomma "Horrid little beast!" But the goat is the children's totem, and they themselves have become containers for bullets—as Dick's dream shows. Terrified of their losses and about to feed on the thorns and roots of the war for success, the children are becoming themselves the beast. The goat who substitutes as a momma for them is also the explosive God-father. Kipling's way of giving the he-goat a female sounding name forecasts the novel's questioning of male and female alike as culturally determined components of the war against failure. Later in the text Dick will utter an apparently unmotivated exclamation against "hermaphroditic futilities." Both this exclamation and the hermaphrodite goat-totem find their appropriate comment in Swinburne on sexual division in Blake: "Contradictory as it may seem . . . the hermaphroditic emblem is always used [by Blake] as a symbol seemingly of duplicity and division, perplexity and restraint. The two sexes should not combine and contend; they must finally amalgamate and be annihilated." In swallowing the world as ammunition, the children are incorporating the duplicity and division that has already beaten them and that will devote them in turn to administering beatings. And although by means of the pastoral grass collar the dream suggests a world outside creative jealousy's modes of order, for Kipling this *is* only a dream, and every worldly, loss-terrified alternative is beastly.

Thus when Kipling repeats or varies "Horrid little beast!" in the second and fourth chapters, the variation harks back to what the goatlike bullet-swallowing children dramatize at the novel's start about the creative jealousy they are not able to escape. To see the "beast" motif or rhyme as an attack on women or as prudery about sex is to read with prejudice, and inflexibly. And like the "beast" motif, the opening chapters' other significant rhymes—all of which use momentary blindness to forecast Dick's loss of sight—repay disinterested attention. Before each of the moments of temporary blindness, Kipling presents Dick focussing on reflections in water or on metal of the setting sun. The sun is always associated with aggressive wrath: "a wrathful red disk" is varied as a "savage red disk" on a spear-point that is "a red splash in the distance," which in the fourth chapter becomes "a blood-red wafer." There is reason to read these repeated suns as figures for the explosive resentment against loss that Dick sees everything in the light of; it is this wrathful light, which is a figure for the creative order of jealousy Dick wants to succeed in, that the novel claims is the light that fails. Like Amomma, the red disk is used by Kipling to compound vivid immediacy with abstract analysis. In the case of the sun-figure, the analysis comes from Kipling's view of imperialism (in this novel)—a view covered up by critical insistence that the wrathful light is only a sign of Maisie's aggression against Dick. When during the second chapter's sunset Dick receives his ultimately blinding injury from a Mahdi attacker, he is also dealing out wounds, and his best friend Torpenhow is using a thumb to put out an Arab's eye. What we might well understand here is that even where the usually noncombatant correspondents are concerned, there is a correspondence between violent imperialist wrath inflicted on native populations and secret, internal wounds these inflictions wreak in turn on the imperialists. During the scene of Dick's desert skirmish, Gordon's death at Khartoum—the failure in the 1880s of British imperialism against the Mahdi—is occurring. But this wounding failure is not represented by Kipling as the pity of an imperialist defeat. In fact Kipling's "moral" is that the infliction of victimhood on the victor (unlike Gordon, Dick's cohorts win their skirmish) is a first opening towards blindness to the world dominated by the jealous order of British success. Eventually, the novel says, the wound of failure opens one to freedom from the creative daemon. If like the Mahdieh Maisie wounds Dick, then the imperialist's native victims are a likeness of Maisie—of woman; she then is the native force whose rebellion has the potential to open the hero to liberation from success—and from the terror of loss.

Once worldly life—figured by the blood-red disk of wrath—fails, what there is to see, and to see in the light of, is what we might call visionary, even though it is an obscurity or darkness from the worldly point of view in which failure is feared and is not acceptable. This obscurity of vision, a twin to the obscurities of failure and of death, is the genuine counterviolence that contrasts with Dick's defensive aggression. Maisie has been criticized for being an agent of this saving counterviolence!—though Kipling's rhymes on Maisie's association with Dick's growing darkness even predict this salvation. When Maisie's hair blows across Dick's face in the first chapter and thereby spoils his aim, Kipling makes the spoiling agent not Maisie but a "thrashing" night-wind—an extension of Mrs. Jennett's Creator and his jealous wrath. The aim that is being spoiled needs to be spoiled since it is an aiming at resentful anger as a vocation. Within two pages of the description of the blinding darkness of Maisie's hair, as the children assert the comfort of belonging to each other, the evening becomes "the kindly darkness [that] hid them both"; and then, when in the fourth chapter, Dick rediscovers Maisie just after the black smoke of a Thames river steamer has obscured his vision, we are reminded—or should be—of the kindly obscurity that has enveloped hero and heroine within mutual belonging. The failure of light, the "rhymes" on darkness suggest, is a loving and saving obscurity.

So, in conjunction with the thematic influence of Blake and Swinburne, the "rhymes" that organize the exposition of Kipling's novel work—when they are read closely—in a way that undoes the customary evaluation and its grounds. And the "rhymes" are an essential part of a formal aspect of

The Light That Failed that has a bearing on Kipling's work in general. One of Kipling's failures, it has been said repeatedly, is his inability to write extended works, novels rather than tales. The possibility that Kipling intended to reform "the novel" in the direction of radical condensation and brevity, that he wanted the customary extent of fiction to fail, and that this intention is the result of his thematic visions and obsessions, is not broached; yet it ought to be. In *The Light That Failed* Kipling describes one of Dick's best paintings as the result of the artist's "going out of my way to foreshorten for sheer delight of doing it." This is a tip to the reader about the method of the novel's composition, and about the delight even the reader might take in the technique.

Kipling's fiction is the development of an art of foreshortening. Although Dick's painting illustrates Poe, a practitioner of the same art, here too Blake and Swinburne are inspirations. Blake foreshortened by his habit of condensing extended psychic and narrative sequences into one simultaneous moment, and Swinburne by his habit of forcing antitheses to become oxymorons. But above all, Kipling's thoughts about failure set the pattern of formal foreshortening for *The Light That Failed,* and they make use of the rhymes as an essential part of the pattern. The rhymes impact Dick's rising career and the novel's rising action upon moments of sunset and decline. By seeming to repeat the novel's start three or four times over via the same details, Kipling produces in the reader a discomfort with the novel's mode of succession. With his initial and initiatory aspects set in a constant glow of sunset, the writer makes the reader sense succession of a linear and temporal sort as blocked, as steps forward that are a mere walking in place. This sense of blocked narrative succession transfers itself back and forth, in a kind of formal pun, between the novel's structure and its theme of success: the latter is from the start not a progress but a stasis, is an ascension in a frozen state of decline. By the third chapter, in fact, before Dick's reunion with Maisie, the hero already has begun to decline. Torpenhow kicks in one of Dick's canvasses in protest against the way success is spoiling Dick's aim. Success is spoiling just because it seems to surmount vulnerability to discontinuity, to loss of effort and life. The unperceived blinding Dick receives in the second chapter shows the omnipresence of the loss that success may appear to overcome, but never will. The succession of achievements called a career is thus an illusory flight from the obscurity environing light and life. What rises at the start of the novel is the setting sun, the intrusiveness of ending, the violence done to moments that succeed each other. Kipling's rhymes surprisingly and paradoxically disjoin the novel's initial and sequential elements, in a way predicting not just the hero's breakup but the text's.

But before we see how Kipling attempts to make the text witness its own demise as a vivid and visual picture of things, Kipling's presentation of Maisie and Bessie needs to be reclaimed as much as his novel's beginning. In their own pursuits of success Maisie and Bessie share the male's terrified reaction to loss; all three compose an hermaphroditic emblem of "duplicity and division," of futilely "jealous love and personal desire." The three characters must be read as emanations of each other; what combines and contends in each are aspects of the other two. Yet even when we do read the characters so, we see that Kipling has furnished Maisie with an aura of integrity of character superior to Dick's. Like Dick, Maisie is terrified by loss and mortality into choosing art as a defense, but she maintains this choice in a less incoherent way than the man. Dick represents for Kipling the incoherence of the male attachment to success; like his knowing male friends, Dick insists he is liberated from success, and harangues Maisie to free herself from its pursuit; but his emotional attachment to what his mind opposes persists, and as a result of his self-contradiction he appears to be more enslaved to success than Maisie. At least Maisie knows what she wants and does not compromise her desire; Dick is all compromise, cannot practice what he preaches, and exhibits even his vaunted liberation as yet another way of beating the world—and Maisie. Having admitted in chapter 5 that "there is too much Ego in my Cosmos," and having made that into a sermon to Maisie on the superiority of craft to worldly success, in chapter 7 (the novel's midpoint) Dick confesses that he still believes the world owes him money and recognition: he can not get over the rancor of having once been down and out in London and of having been cheated then of threepence he never got for carrying a man's bags. Maisie teases Dick into confessing his stubborn resentment of failure, hence his persisting worship of success; and then she playfully restores the lost threepence out of her own pocket. "The very human apostle of fair craft" takes the coin though it is not "befitting the man who had preached the sanctity of work." Kipling sets this confession at exactly the seaside scene of the early pistol-shooting, to remind us of the origins of Dick's career in anger fixated on loss. And then when Dick takes the "restored" coin and throws it into the Thames, we learn that the coin's drowning "seemed to cut him free from thought of Maisie for the moment." So Maisie is for Dick the coin he has not gotten out of the world; thereby his solicitations of her in the name of love remain the token of his war for success, against vulnerability. His "love"—which he usually feels as pity for her bad habits and lack of talent—seems a self-deceiving compunction for a kind of secret violence he keeps doing her. Although grown-up Maisie has told Dick forthrightly that she neither loves him nor wants to, he refuses to take her honesty to heart—refuses, that is, to take her loss to heart. "The end was only a question of time now," he thinks, "and the prize well worth the waiting." And while he waits, he proposes a competition: they will each paint a figure of Melancolia as it appears in "The City of Dreadful Night," and they will see who better succeeds at the portrayal. We find Dick swearing—in a way that is funny at his own expense—"I'll make her understand that I can beat her on her own Melancolia." It's just this order of beatings that produces the melancholy order of things Kipling portrays.

Maisie seems stronger than Dick, less liable to beat others (*and* less liable to succeed) just because she is able not to confuse her fear of loss, her desire for success, or her pity, with love. Maisie's last appearance in the novel is when Torpenhow brings her back from France to England, in a rather callous attempt to palm blind Dick off on her. While she has been abroad, Maisie has begun to suspect that Dick is helping someone else to paint, so she has grown jealous to the point of thinking that she is after all "in love with him." Faced with Dick's invalidism, she is on the verge of feeling the love Los and Enitharmon feel whenever one sees the other wounded. This is just the kind of "love" Dick's male friends are feeling for him—a fact curiously not faced by those who claim the novel idealizes male friendship. Since the men consider Dick a failure now—"out of the race,—down,—*gastados*, expended, finished, done for"—they must get rid of him, so that their own work will not be hampered. They assume that woman's place is to "love" pitiful dropouts from the all-important success they pursue—even though like Dick the friends preach craft for craft's sake while they practice craft for unhampered success's sake. But, in spite of the friends' considerable pressure on her to take a "selfless" place in the world of male success, Maisie resists. She is horrified by Dick's blindness, but we are told she does not confuse things as the men do: "she was only filled with pity most startlingly distinct from love." Maisie's ability to keep love and pity distinct gives her a clear-sighted integrity that no man in the novel possesses—and that the hero will not possess until he has got used to being blind.

Bessie Broke, like Maisie, is another of the aspects that combine and contend in Dick. This other member of the hermaphrodite trinity also has a coherence superior to the male's. Following what he has done with Maisie, Kipling uses Bessie as a touchstone for the reader's view of Dick's confusions. In painting the Melancolia, Dick makes the face of the portrait a composite of Maisie's and Bessie's faces. This detail has aptness when we think of the origin of the picture in Dick's "pique"—as he calls it—against Maisie. The prostitute's role in the composite face asks to be read as a likeness for Dick's attempt to prostitute Maisie to his will to succeed as her lover. Kipling in his foreshortening way is also showing that the prostitute's role in the picture is a sign of Dick's own continuing prostitution to the public success which Dick says he despises even as he makes Maisie a stand-in for it. Choosing to make Bessie destroy the Melancolia, Kipling is picturing the way the prostitution and the coercion that produce art ruin it. Of course, Bessie spoils the painting since Dick has spoiled her masterpiece, the housekeeping she had aimed to set up with Torpenhow. Dick insists on packing off Torpenhow because he claims the latter's affair with Bessie will spoil for good the foreign correspondence; but Dick has recently been preaching the fatheadedness of believing in lasting work, and he already has asked Maisie to run off to the tropics on the assumption that domesticity anywhere will not interfere with art. As the victim of this incoherence, Bessie, who fully knows what *she* wants, has a right to avenge herself. The Bessie-part of his own self is racking Dick here, and his ultimate freedom from his contradictions is actually helped along by Bessie's justifiable adversity.

But while the novel shows the women in a better light than it shows the man, *The Light That Failed* does not endorse the success either the man or the women pursue. And whether the pursuit is aesthetically or domestically oriented, whether unconventionally or conventionally, the novel's claim is that all pursuits of success grind at the same terror-driven mill. Out of the desire for compensation for loss and out of pity Dick in his blindness proposes marriage to Bessie, but this would be a way of sitting down to the marriage feast in "secret discontent and scorn." And in contrast to Maisie, Bessie confuses pity for Dick with love; her domestic ambitions are her rancorous way of collecting threepence from the world. When Dick breaks off the marriage, he is no longer acting incoherently—he would be continuing to act incoherently only if he pursued the marriage. We are to understand that his blindness and the destruction of his work have brought him to believe that even marriage abets the structure of self-contradiction that is the order of creative jealousy. Neither the work of art nor the work of marriage can succeed against darkness, because aesthetic and domestic order remain within the pale of displaced defensive rage. We perhaps can see Kipling himself coming more definitely to his novel's idea about marriage by means of a striking fact in the publication history of *The Light That Failed*. Within five months Kipling published two versions of the book, the second of which he declared was the story "as it was originally conceived." The second is the version we have; the first appeared in America in *Lippincott's* magazine, is shorter, and ends happily, with Maisie marrying the blind hero. It is possible the magazine asked for changes in the "original" harsh story; it is also said that Kipling's mother asked him for a more pleasant finale. Yet, in line with the criticism of success, the marriage in the "happy" version is presented as a liberating escape from the success Dick's fellow journalists pursue, with what is shown to be coarse self-confidence. But in the months before the English appearance of the novel, what may have come clear to Kipling was that the privacy of marriage—any domestic arrangements, in fact—could not escape the social order's devotion to beating loss.

As a way of demonstrating the logic of his vision and, hence, of the inescapable link between domestic order and a society founded on beating failure, Kipling entwines Dick's last phase with Bessie with a sudden focus on the family of Dick's landlord, the Beetons. Beeton and his wife steal from Dick things they insist are useless to a blind man; in exchange they send their boy Alf to minister to Dick. The Beetons pin their hopes for worldly success on Alf, a talented mimic whose receptivity to education and whose sentimentality about domestic order are highly promising of worldly achievement. "He do read beautiful, seeing he's only nine" and "only to 'ear Alf sing 'A Boy's Best Friend is 'is Mother'! Ah!" the parents exclaim. The Beetons are a version of what Dick has been, and what London relies on for stability while Britain attempts to succeed in mastering the world. And Kipling suggests that Alf is what he himself is or has been—and what Dick and Kipling together must leave behind. The novel's publication in its original form begins with dedicatory verses, apparently to Kipling's mother, that might as well carry the title of Alf's song. If Mrs. Kipling urged the bowdlerized version of the novel in *Lippincott's*, presumably this ending gave the novel a better chance at worldly success. But in publishing the novel's unhappy ending Kipling makes it obvious that he does not want to underwrite the dictates of success. The dedicatory poem both asserts and subverts the novelist's possible identification with Alf by a sly equivocation: the "mother o'mine" in the verse's refrain could be *Swinburne's* sea, the sea that brings liberty and destruction together and that Dick talks about in Swinburnian terms in the novel's eighth chapter, which also was not published in *Lippincott's*. Bessie Broke, the Beetons, and Mrs. Kipling too, want to defeat loss with a form of domestic success that for Kipling is already broken and failed by its dependence on beatings, both at home and abroad. Because we are asked to see this order as inescapable, Dick does not take up the opportunity of marriage with Maisie's friend, a jealous yet admiring impressionist painter. In his final trip to Africa, the novel's hero steps out altogether from the order of creative jealousy.

The surrender to loss means for the artist Kipling—and not just for the artist Dick—an insistence on the failure and mortality of all picturings of the world. To insist on any surmounting of failure by the success of creative articulation would endorse the order of things the novel criticizes. *The Light That Failed* does not evade facing its own consequent paradox: it offers its readers an urgent abstract vision of the world in a vivid verbal mode of picturing things, at the same time as it calls into question the accuracy and trustworthiness of its very mode of envisioning. The novel—and the novelist—must enact their own self-blinding to point beyond that order of creative jealousy in which even the delineations of art are defensively imbedded. Whatever the psychoanalytical dimensions and motivations of this may be, the historical dimensions and motivations are fully set out by Kipling. To the surprise of our prejudices about him, he suggests that art must undergo and face its own blinding in order to be saved from, above all, alliance with the imperialist aspect of creative jealousy. Kipling ties his Blakeian and Swinburnian vision to concrete history in order to resist the ties his own work has with the Beetons. They intend to command the future by a surprising alliance with art, because for them art clarifies obscurity, and its picturings enlighten, in a way that serves their self-aggrandizing power. In the world of the Beetons, that is, the Beetons together with artists like Maisie and Dick want art to succeed against obscurity, want art's contemplations to invent the world as an intelligible place, not as a place of violence done to clarity and articulation. In such invention there is a defense against loss; success then is picturing (especially in Kipling's own vivid mode), success is articulation itself. "Whether Gordon lived or died, or half the British army went to pieces in the sand" does not matter, as the special correspondents know; what matters is that "The Soudan Campaign was a picturesque one, and lent itself to vivid word-painting. . . . All [the masses] demanded was picturesqueness and abundance of detail." "Amused and thrilled and interested" by the success of portrayal, "England at breakfast" (identified as "Lover of Justice, Constant Reader, Paterfamilias, and all that lot") can withstand the loss of Gordon, because at least the special correspondents have beaten the darkness. They have brought to the eyes of England, in the form of thrilling delineations, the Mahdi natives themselves. Like the artists with whom they remain in close alliance, the special correspondents in Kipling's novel testify to the way in which confidently articulated mediation of the world is expected to be an ally against loss.

To oppose this alliance against loss makes Kipling not want to identify his art with such special correspondence. The confidence in what the artist can see or can make visible is a blind for the artist's situation in the imperialist order of creative jealousy. Kipling's analysis of the artist's tie to imperialist success pervades his youthful work. We see it in the same year as *The Light That Failed* in a story called "A Conference of the Powers," where the celebrated novelist Eustace Cleever discovers that his clever art fails to articulate or even suggest the experience in India of a young soldier called the Infant. Yet for Cleever to succeed here would amount to a treacherous domination of the Infant who is an indomitable object of wonder because he has not been and can not be articulated. And when the Infant tells a story about a Burmese native, Boh Na-ghee, we see that the Boh is to the Infant what the latter is to the novelist: an impenetrable but awesome obscurity. The Infant can only lisp about the Boh, but just this saves the Boh from being mastered by the imperializing success of portrayal. Even in the Stalky series, "The Flag of Their Country" (1899) presents another version of Cleever in the figure of the M.P. whose confident clarity about the Empire's servants and its governed peoples is reprehensible to Kipling.

It is clarity itself that the creative order of jealousy has made reprehensible, so that Kipling must play Bessie Broke to his own work, rubbing out his own canvasses. The way to rub out melancolia rooted in the fear of loss, Kipling seems to think, is to join with loss to exhibit articulation's failures. This violent self-impairment of the artist and his work is the counterviolence that must be done to the Creator-daemon, to his defensive aggression. There is only one moment in *The Light That Failed* which sharply contradicts Kipling's identification with violence committed against creative jealousy. When Dick hears that Bessie has destroyed his work, the narrative asserts that a man, unlike a woman, "will never forgive the destruction of his work." The statement is perhaps a sign of Kipling's resistance to the bowdlerizing of his novel, but it is also perhaps a sign of his joining with his aggressors in the name of success. Whatever its motive, the assertion is both artistically and sexually offensive because the rest of the novel belies it. Neither Maisie nor Bessie forgive the destruction of their work, considered either as art or as domesticity; but it is just this lack of forgiveness for such destruction, rather than destruction itself, which the novel refuses to countenance in women and men alike. Perhaps it would be more accurate to say that Kipling must play not Bessie but the female impressionist to his work, for Maisie's friend provides a model of accepting destruction of one's art. Dick has long felt guilty for the way he has mastered his human subjects—"all the people in the past whom he had laid open for the purpose of his own craft." One day he is "laid open" in turn by Maisie's friend, whose accuracy of portrayal is a way of mocking and beating Dick. Yet the impressionist deliberately destroys her sketch of Dick, both to save him pain and to surrender her own defensive aggression—for she is bitterly jealous (another hermaphroditic futility) of Dick and Maisie.

Again, then, a woman is the model for what Kipling must do to his own art—make it surrender its ambition to master the world by submitting to the vulnerability and mortality that are feared by mastery. Art must be brought to view the place where it fails, the borderline site where it can not even articulate an object. At this borderline art's ventures are sunsets; they are exposed as thresholds of loss. Yet this thresholding is not to be lamented; the violence of loss and failure art undergoes in *The Light That Failed* is the only possible counter to jealousy. So not just the impressionist, but Dick and Torpenhow actively destroy their work, and suffer and forgive the destruction. In the eighth chapter Dick tells without regret the story of the loss of what had been his best work: a fantasy of Poe's "Annabel Lee" done on the walls of a hold of a ship long since sunk and hence triumphed over by that "mother o'mine," the sea. In the same chapter we are told of Dick's sketchbook in which satiric cartoons portray the life of a special correspondent called by the name of a Sudanese tribe, the Nilghai. Although the sketchbook is copiously and wildly inventive, we are told that Dick cannot—and will not—portray the most important event in the life of the Nilghai; like the Boh's, the heart of the Nilghai can't be penetrated by portrayal. Even the artist's power of conviction about what he cannot articulate or about the vulnerable dignity of his craft can not secure for his work any foregoing of the violence of loss it must accept. The talk in the novel about the importance to art of convictions is a red herring; neither convictions, nor will, nor hard work guarantee any surmounting of failure and death.

Summarizing the "moral" of Blake's portrait of the blind artist Milton, Swinburne writes, "Only by vision or by death shall we be brought safe past the watch guarded by the sentinels of material form and bodily life, the crude tributary 'Afrites' (as in the Aeschylean myth) of the governing power which fashions and fetters life." For *The Light That Failed* "the sentinels of material form and bodily life" are the thresholds art must designate as such, to show the obscurity of what lies beyond the sentinels, even though the demonstration costs the "governing power" not just of art but of historical life, even of psychosexual life. If art is to have justification, *The Light That Failed* suggests that its defense can lie in its vulnerable attempt to point out the contradictions in which the Empire's art and experience together are trapped by their terror of loss. Interestingly, it is the "Afrites" whom the British want to make tributary who lead Dick out of the fabrications and fetters of material life and western success; it is the Mahdieh, whose leader is a mystic visionary, impenetrable by western eyes, and the Mahdieh's violence done to the Empire's light and power that bring Dick "past the watch." The last strikingly vivid picture of *The Light That Failed*, the last one Kipling delineates and also rubs out in order to end his text, conveys a powerfully darkened Blakeian vision—something like an assertion that "only by obscurity of vision and by death can we be safe." The picture epitomizes the careless violence Kipling suggests must be done to vivid aesthetic picturings, to free them from the world's jealous fetters, and to make them faithful to an obscure but trustworthy alternative to the world.

In the novel's finale blind Dick has made his way back to the Sudan, and rides an armored troop train, looking like "one long coffin," out to Suakin; from there he commandeers a camel and a camel driver to take him to an outpost where he hopes to find Torpenhow. So as not to be tricked, he must ride the camel with a gun in the driver's back. Half-asleep atop the camel, revolver in hand, he hallucinates he is learning "a punishment hymn" at Mrs. Jennett's. But the only lines in the hymn he can learn are about deliverance, because he is being delivered from the order of creative jealousy. The image of this deliverance is marked by a shift in his hallucination: he thinks he is back in London, picturing on canvas the desert scene that is blindly before him:

> The last hour before the light lengthens itself into many eternities. It seemed to Dick that he had never since the beginning of original darkness done anything at all save jolt through the air. Once in a thousand years he would finger the nailheads on the saddle-front and count them all carefully. Centuries later he would shift his revolver from his right hand to his left and allow the eased arm to drop down at his side. From the safe distance of London he was watching himself thus employed,—watching critically. Yet whenever he put out his hand to the canvas that he might paint the tawny yellow desert under the glare of the sinking moon, the black shadow of the camel and the two bowed figures atop, that hand held a revolver and the arm was numbed from wrist to collar-bone. Moreover, he was in the dark, and could see no canvas of any kind whatever.

There is great summary power here for Kipling's thematic and formal intentions. At the moment when the writer is picturing for us the blind man's ride in the desert, he reminds us of how difficult it is to see once one has traveled beyond the place where picturing has its capital in the world of success. Yet this traveling into the eternities of darkness is necessary just because it remains out of the reach of the artist's eye, arm, and aim. The attempt to delineate or articulate the darkness that lies on the other side of creative jealousy can only do defensive violence to that darkness; commanded by such enlightening intention, the artist's art is a form of imperialism, a gun in the back of what is beyond the empire's sentinels and front lines. Dick has harassed Maisie to "go on with your line-work," but neither color nor line has any capability of correspondence with the obscurity that must spoil all lines. Like the brush or the pen, the "creative" weapons that succeed in the worldly London distance, the revolver here is what it was in the novel's first chapter: the aggressive instrument, using terror as a defense against terror. But the rhyme of the revolver here with the earlier pistol-practice also bears a different meaning. The gun is rendered impotent because the numbness of the wrist holding it is the sign of vulnerability—of the mind's and the body's vulnerability to failure and loss, which no creative act can overcome. The revolver memorializes the defensiveness that for Dick is past. And now that the worldly canvass can not be seen in any light whatsoever, now that it is no longer the scene to which Dick's ambition is attached, the revolver also figures the nondefensive, careless violence with which Dick is joined. It is a violence that enacts loss, that actively takes the side of mortality by abetting death's work. His mortality gives Dick the energy to carry through this last adventure in the desert. The death that succeeds the adventure is, of course, a suicide, which under western eyes has long been held to be unacceptable as a sane, voluntary, and not shameful act. For the young visionary Kipling it seems that salvific human possibilities other than the acceptable ones needed to be pursued, at no matter what violent cost to history, to selves, and to creative art.

Like Dick Heldar, in *Dispatches* Errol Flynn's son Sean, one of Michael Herr's most admired fellow "specials," disappears into the darkness, never to be seen again. Was he a "victim" to "something more complicated than death" or merely free from the fear of death? In contrast to Flynn, Herr retreats from loss to America and "success," even at the expense of what he seems on the verge of seeing as an identity between success and the war that is on, all the time. The sadly notable thing about Kipling, of course, is that he too may have retreated from his vision of failure after *The Light That Failed.* Perhaps the subsequent events of Kipling's life—the deaths of two of his three children especially—tested the novel's implications with so unremitting a pressure that Kipling could no longer face what young strength had given him the pessimism to see. In his subsequent worldly politics he may have capitulated to a resistance to all the darkness of failure. Nevertheless, the later work does not put aside and cancel the thematics and poetics of *The Light That Failed,* no matter what Kipling's life put aside. And Kipling's life does not matter to his work or to his literary tradition. Loss without compensation and failure as a redress to the world of creative beatings continue to show themselves in Kipling's writing. And just as more needs to be said about the writing, so more needs to be said about Kipling's literary roots (I have not even mentioned Browning); and much more about the tradition Kipling made rather than the tradition he was made by. How long, for example, will it be still possible to ignore Kipling's influence on Conrad? We have celebrated *Heart of Darkness*'s venture into the blinding of vision without a thought of Kipling; yet Conrad published an unsigned article on him in *Outlook* in April 1898; and the curious detail that turns up a painting by Kurtz at the Congo Central Station may owe itself to the Melancolia. Kurtz's painting is of an allegorical blindfolded woman carrying a lighted torch, a picture that forecasts Marlow's adventure as a study of a light that has failed and as an enactment of sight's replacement by impenetrable obscurity. Before he writes *Heart of Darkness* Conrad proclaims the artist's duty as "before all, to make you see," in apparent contrast to Kipling's assertion that the artist's task, before all, is to darken sight, to make your sight fail. Yet when Conrad comes to his Congo story, it is as if he has changed his mind about the artist's task, and is following Kipling. We keep ourselves from seeing this sort of influence by dismissing *The Light That Failed* as a failure. But it is with an ironic appropriateness to his work that we continue to maintain our loss of Kipling.

Chronology

<table>
<tr><td>1865</td><td>Rudyard Kipling born on December 30 in Bombay, son of Alice and John Lockwood Kipling.</td></tr>
<tr><td>1871–77</td><td>Spends this unhappy period as a boarder at the "House of Desolation" in Southsea.</td></tr>
<tr><td>1878–82</td><td>Attends United Services College.</td></tr>
<tr><td>1882–87</td><td>Reporter for The Civil and Military Gazette, Lahore.</td></tr>
<tr><td>1886</td><td>Departmental Ditties.</td></tr>
<tr><td>1887–89</td><td>On the staff of The Pioneer, Allahabad.</td></tr>
<tr><td>1888</td><td>Plain Tales from the Hills published, followed by the other Indian Railways Series titles: Soldiers Three, The Story of the Gadsby's, In Black and White, Wee Willie Winkie, The Phantom Rickshaw, Under the Deodars.</td></tr>
<tr><td>1889</td><td>Returns to London, via Japan and America. Sea to Sea.</td></tr>
<tr><td>1890</td><td>Indian Railway Series reprinted. The Light That Failed.</td></tr>
<tr><td>1891</td><td>Life's Handicap. Voyage to South Africa, Australia, New Zealand, and, for the last time, India.</td></tr>
<tr><td>1892</td><td>Marriage to Caroline Balestier. The Naulahka. Barrack-Room Ballads. Honeymoon journey through Canada to Japan. Returns to his wife's home in Brattleboro, Vermont.</td></tr>
<tr><td>1893</td><td>Many Inventions.</td></tr>
<tr><td>1894</td><td>The Jungle Book.</td></tr>
<tr><td>1895</td><td>The Second Jungle Book.</td></tr>
</table>

1896   *The Seven Seas*, poems. Kipling quarrels with his brother-in-law (who was also his agent) and he and his wife leave Vermont for England.

1897   *Captains Courageous*. Settles in Rottingdean.

1898   *The Day's Work*.

1899   *Stalky & Co.* Kipling makes his last visit to America. Josephine, his eldest child, dies.

1900–1908   Spends January to March in South Africa every year.

1901   *Kim*.

1902   *Just So Stories*. Moves to "Bateman's," Sussex.

1903   *The Five Nations*, poems.

1904   *Traffics and Discoveries*.

1906   *Puck of Pook's Hill*.

1907   Awarded the Nobel Prize for literature.

1909   *Actions and Reactions*.

1910   *Rewards and Fairies*.

1913   Voyage to Egypt. *Letters of Travel. Songs from Books.*

1915   Kipling's son, John, missing and believed killed in France.

1917   *A Diversity of Creatures*.

1919   *The Years Between*.

1923   *Land and Sea Tales for Scouts and Guides. The Irish Guards in the Great War.*

1926   *Debits and Credits*.

1927   Voyage to Brazil. *Brazilian Sketches*.

1930   *Thy Servant a Dog*. Voyage to West Indies.

1932   *Limits and Renewals*.

1936   Rudyard Kipling dies on January 18, in London.

1937   *Something of Myself*, an autobiography, published posthumously.

Contributors

HAROLD BLOOM, Sterling Professor of the Humanities at Yale University, is the author of *The Anxiety of Influence*, *Poetry and Repression*, and many other volumes of literary criticism. His forthcoming study, *Freud: Transference and Authority*, attempts a full-scale reading of all of Freud's major writings. A MacArthur Prize Fellow, he is general editor of five series of literary criticism published by Chelsea House.

RANDALL JARRELL, poet, novelist, critic, and essayist, was Professor of English at Sarah Lawrence College. His books of essays and criticism include *Poetry and the Age*, *Poets, Critics, and Readers*, and *Kipling, Auden & Co.*

ANGUS WILSON is Professor of English at East Anglia University. His books include *The Strange Ride of Rudyard Kipling*, *The World of Charles Dickens*, and a study of Zola's novels.

IRVING HOWE is Distinguished Professor of English at Hunter College. His best-known book is *World of Our Fathers*. He is also known for his studies of Faulkner, Hardy, and Sherwood Anderson.

DONALD DAVIE is Professor of English at Vanderbilt University. His books include *Purity of Diction in English Verse*, *Thomas Hardy and British Poetry*, and two studies of Ezra Pound.

ZOHREH T. SULLIVAN is Assistant Professor of English at the University of Illinois, Champaign-Urbana. She has written articles on other British authors, including Iris Murdoch, and contributes frequently to *Modern Fiction Studies* and the *Journal of Narrative Technique*.

DAVID BROMWICH is Associate Professor of English at Princeton University. He is the author of *Hazlitt: The Mind of the Critic* and of many essays on contemporary poetry.

ELLIOT L. GILBERT is Professor of English at the University of California, Davis. He is the author of *The Good Kipling* and editor of *Kipling and the Critics*, a collection of essays on Kipling.

ROBERT L. CASERIO is Associate Professor of English at Oberlin College. He is the author of *Plot, Story and the Novel: From Dickens and Poe to the Modern Period*.

Bibliography

Amis, Kingsley. *Rudyard Kipling and His World*. London: Thames & Hudson, 1975.

Auden, W. H. "The Poet of the Encirclement." *The New Republic* 109 (1943): 579–81.

Babbitt, Irving. "Romanticism and the Orient." *Bookman* 74 (December 1931): 352–54.

Bodelsen, C. A. *Aspects of Kipling's Art*. New York: Barnes & Noble, 1964.

Bratton, Jacqueline S. "Kipling's Magic Art." *Proceedings of the British Academy* 64 (1968): 209–32.

Chaudhuri, Nirad C. "The Finest Story about India—in English." *Encounter* 7 (April 1957): 47–53.

Dobree, Bonamy. "Kipling the Visionary." *Kipling Journal* 23 (April 1956): 3–5.

———. *Rudyard Kipling: Realist and Fabulist*. London: Oxford University Press, 1972.

Draudt, Manfred. "Reality or Delusion? Narrative Technique and Meaning in Kipling's *The Man Who Would Be King*." *English Studies* 65, no. 4 (August 1984): 316–26.

Eliot, T. S. *A Choice of Kipling's Verse*. London: Faber, 1941.

Gilbert, Elliot L. *The Good Kipling*. Athens: Ohio University Press, 1972.

———. "Silence and Survival in Rudyard Kipling's Art and Life." *English Literature in Transition* 29, no. 2 (1986): 115–26.

———, ed. *Kipling and the Critics*. New York: New York University Press, 1965.

Gross, John, ed. *Rudyard Kipling: The Man, His Work and His World*. London: Weidenfeld & Nicolson, 1972.

Islam, Shamsul. "The Kipling and Hemingway Codes: A Study in Comparison." *Explorations* 2, no. 2 (Winter 1975): 22–28.

———. *Kipling's "Law": A Study of His Philosophy of Life*. London: Macmillan, 1975.

———. *Chronicles of the Raj: A Study of Literary Reaction to the Imperial Idea towards the End of the Raj*. London: Macmillan, 1979.

Jarrell, Randall. *Kipling, Auden & Co.: Essays and Reviews 1935–1964*. New York: Farrar, Straus & Giroux, 1961.

Lewis, C. S. "Kipling's World." In *Literature and Life: Addresses to the English Association*, edited by H. Idris Bell et al. 1948. Reprint. Millwood, N.Y.: Associated Faculty Press, 1970.

McLuhan, Herbert Marshall. "Kipling and Forster." *The Sewanee Review* 52, no. 3 (Summer 1944): 332–43.

Mason, Philip. *Kipling: The Glass, the Shadow and the Fire*. London: Jonathon Cape, 1975.

Meyers, Jeffrey. "The Idea of Moral Authority in *The Man Who Would Be King*." *Studies in English Literature 1500–1900* 8, no. 4 (Autumn 1968): 711–23.

Moore, Katharine. *Kipling and the White Man's Burden*. London: Faber, 1968.

Norton, Charles Eliot. "The Poetry of Rudyard Kipling." *The Atlantic Monthly* 79 (January 1897): 111–15.

Orwell, George. "Rudyard Kipling." *Dickens, Dali and Others*. New York: Harcourt, Brace & World, 1946.

Packard, Winthrop. "Rudyard Kipling: An Estimate." *National Magazine* 10 (April 1899): 77–79.

Roskies, D. M. E. "Telling the Truth about Kipling and Freud." *English* 31, no. 139 (Spring 1982): 1–17.

Rutherford, Andrew, ed. *Kipling's Mind and Art*. Stanford: Stanford University Press, 1964.

Scheerer, Constance. "The Lost Paradise of Rudyard Kipling." *Dalhousie Review* 61, no. 1 (Spring 1981): 27–36.

Seed, David. "Disorientation and Commitment in the Fiction of Empire: Kipling and Orwell." *The Dutch Quarterly Review* 14, no. 4 (1984): 269–80.

Shahane, Vasant A. *Rudyard Kipling, Activist and Artist*. Carbondale: Southern Illinois University Press, 1973.

Shanks, Edward. *Rudyard Kipling: A Study in Literature and Political Ideas*. New York: Doubleday, Doran, 1940.

Shippey, Thomas A., and Michael Short. "Framing and Distancing in Kipling's *The Man Who Would Be King*." *The Journal of Narrative Technique* 2, no. 2 (May 1972): 75–87.

Stevenson, Lionel. "The Ideas in Kipling's Poetry." *University of Toronto Quarterly* 1 (July 1932): 467–89.

Stewart, J. I. M. *Rudyard Kipling*. New York: Dodd, Mead, 1966.

———. "Fluid at the Centre." *Encounter* 45, no. 3 (Spring 1975): 62–66.

Tomkins, J. M. S. *The Art of Rudyard Kipling*. London: Methuen, 1959.

Trilling, Lionel. *The Liberal Imagination*. New York: Viking, 1951.

Wilson, Edmund. *The Wound and the Bow*. New York: Oxford University Press, 1959.

Yeats, A. W. "The Genesis of 'The Recessional.' " *University of Texas Studies in English* 31 (1952): 97–108.

———. "Kipling, Twenty Years After." *Dalhousie Review* 36 (1956): 59–64.

Acknowledgments

"On Preparing to Read Kipling" by Randall Jarrell from *Kipling, Auden & Co.: Essays and Reviews, 1935–1964* by Randall Jarrell, © 1961 by Randall Jarrell. Reprinted by permission of Farrar, Straus & Giroux.

"*Kim* and the Stories" by Angus Wilson from *The Strange Ride of Rudyard Kipling* by Angus Wilson, © 1977 by Angus Wilson. Reprinted by permission of Viking Penguin, Inc., and Curtis Brown Ltd.

"The Pleasures of *Kim*" by Irving Howe from *Art, Politics, and Will: Essays in Honor of Lionel Trilling*, edited by Quentin Anderson, Stephen Donadio, and Steven Marcus, © 1977 by Basic Books, Inc. Reprinted by permission.

"A Puritan's Empire: The Case of Kipling" by Donald Davie from *The Sewanee Review* 87, no. 1 (Winter 1979), © 1979 by Donald Davie. Reprinted by permission of the editor.

"Kipling the Nightwalker" by Zohreh T. Sullivan from *Modern Fiction Studies* 30, no. 2 (Summer 1984), © 1984 by the Purdue Research Foundation. Reprinted by permission of the Purdue Research Foundation, West Lafayette, Indiana.

"Kipling's Jest" by David Bromwich from *Grand Street* 4, no. 2 (Winter 1985), © 1985 by David Bromwich and Grand Street Publications, Inc. Reprinted by permission.

"Silence and Survival in Kipling's Art and Life" (originally entitled "Silence and Survival in Rudyard Kipling's Art and Life") by Elliot L. Gilbert from *English Literature in Transition, 1880–1920* 29, no. 2 (1986), © 1986 by Elliot L. Gilbert. Reprinted by permission.

"Kipling in the Light of Failure" by Robert L. Caserio from *Grand Street* 6, no. 1 (Fall 1986), © 1986 by Robert L. Caserio and Grand Street Publications, Inc. Reprinted by permission.

Index